"But They Can't Beat Us"

*Oscar Robertson and the
Crispus Attucks Tigers*

by

Randy Roberts

Sports Publishing Inc.
www.SportsPublishingInc.com

Indiana Historical Society
www.indianahistory.org

© 1999 Indiana Historical Society

Director of Production: Susan M. McKinney
Cover and photo insert design: Julie L. Denzer
Editor: David Hamburg

ISBN: 1-57167-257-5

SPORTS PUBLISHING INC.
804 N. Neil St.
Champaign, IL 61820
www.SportsPublishingInc.com

Printed in the United States.

To Alison and Kelly, with all their daddy's love.

———————————————

Contents

Introduction

"You can take your wars and your starvation and your fires and your floods, but there's no heartbreak in life like losing the big game in high school."

—Dan Jenkins, *Semi-Tough*

Nobody could do it all on a basketball court like Oscar Robertson. He could score from inside or outside, rebound and pass, and play defense. As a college player at the University of Cincinnati he led the nation in scoring his sophomore, junior, and senior years. As a professional with the Cincinnati Royals he averaged a triple-double during the 1961–62 season, and for his first five seasons in the National Basketball Association he averaged 30.3 points, 10.4 rebounds, and 10.6 assists per game. Today, any player who achieves two or three triple-doubles during a season is proclaimed a superstar. For Oscar it was just an *average* outing.

"But They Can't Beat Us" is the story of Oscar Robertson's career at Crispus Attucks High School in Indianapolis, Indiana. It may seem oddly out of proportion to write a book about his high school days. One might ask if it wasn't just a prelude to his college and professional careers, to the time when he performed on the national stage. Well, it was and it wasn't. Yes, it was a prelude. By the time Oscar finished his college career in 1960 his name and face were recognized by everyone with even the faint-

est familiarity with the game of basketball. But his high school career is a story in and of itself—a story of race and America, of discrimination and accomplishment, of power and powerlessness, and why the two are not always as simple as they seem. It is a story of Indiana and of basketball, the story of a game played against the backdrop of shadows, but with the ability to illuminate a moment in history. In his college and professional careers Robertson played before more people and earned more fame and fortune. But the stakes were never higher than when he represented Crispus Attucks, the rewards never greater, the issues never more clear-cut. Crispus Attucks was his team, its supporters his people, and winning and losing never had more meaning.

During the research and writing of this book I received support and encouragement from many people. Some shared their memories with me. Bailey Robertson Sr., Yvonne Robertson, Russell Bell, Bill Scott, Edgar Searcy, Ray Crowe, Bill Swatts, Albert Spurlock, Joe Wolfla, Glenn Sample, Ray Craft, Vic Klinker, Ed Jucker, and several followers of Crispus Attucks basketball who wished to remain anonymous added depth to what the sportswriters and editorialists wrote in the 1950s. Several of my graduate students at Purdue University also helped me. Jason Tetzloff, Ed Krzemienski, Chris Elzey, and especially Aram Goudsouzian went beyond the call of duty. The staff at the Indiana Historical Society could not have been more supportive. From Robert M. Taylor Jr.'s initial letter and the editorial work of J. Kent Calder, George Hanlin, Paula Corpuz, Kathy Breen, and Shirley McCord to the handling of countless details by Thomas A. Mason and Ray E. Boomhower, I have enjoyed my time with these professionals. Larry Pitts and Stanley Warren have also been tireless friends of the project. To all these generous people, thanks.

Oscar Robertson, however, deserves the most thanks. He took time from his busy schedule to answer hundreds of questions. He gave thoughtful answers, never pat responses, and insisted throughout that he was just one player on a team of gifted athletes.

On a personal level, my twin daughters Alison and Kelly, now age ten, did not help with the research or provide many insights into Indiana basketball, though they did occasionally turn down the Backstreet Boys or Limp Bizkit long enough to ask me a question or two about Oscar. But they were constant reminders about what is most important and what really matters. Through them, I have felt more connected to Oscar Robertson and his story. This book is dedicated to them.

THE SHOT

In the stands above the Anderson bench people exchanged glances and smiled, as if to say it was about what they expected. There were no doubts now; they would win this 1951 regional title game, take advantage of a weak semifinal division, then capture their fourth state championship. Not that their opponent, with a record of 23-1, hadn't provided a few tense moments. Midway through the second quarter the Crispus Attucks Tigers, the all-black team from the west side of Indianapolis, had led the Anderson Indians 45-30, but that lead had narrowed to 45-37 at the half. Then in the second half the Indians had slowed down Attucks's fast-break game, hit their own shots, taken advantage of several "suspicious" calls by the referees, and moved into the lead. Anderson led by five at the end of the third quarter and by ten with only four and a half minutes left in the game. Even the Attucks supporters, the sea of black faces stuffed into a corner of Indianapolis's Butler Fieldhouse, seemed to have accepted the inevitable. "There was simply no way those black kids were going to win," remembered an Anderson fan.[1]

To make matters worse, John "Noon" Davis, Crispus Attucks's fine forward, had just been called for his fifth foul. His head bent and shoulders rounded, he slouched to the bench, hardly exchanging a word with his substitute, 5'9" sophomore Bailey "Flap" Robertson. In the stands, a smattering of polite applause mixed with shouts of encouragement from the Attucks corner.

Nobody was really sure how Bailey got pegged with the name "Flap." Some said it was the direct result of his loose-wristed shooting and running style. There was an exaggerated pronation and forward extension about his shot. "It was like he was waving at the ball as it left for the hoop," recalled his friend Bill Scott. "And when he ran his hand just kept flappin'." Bill Swatts, another friend from Flap's high school days, was not so sure about the shooting theory. He recalled hearing that Bailey had gotten the name as a result of the old sneakers he used to wear: "We were poor kids. Our parents couldn't afford new shoes. We'd wear them off our feet. Sometimes the lower rubber section would split from the upper canvas part. We'd just wrap them with tape." But the quick playground fix never lasted long, and soon the upper and lower would gape like an open mouth and start flapping as the player ran. Anyway, that's how Swatts believed Bailey got his name. But he admitted there is still another theory that might be true. "Bailey was a talker. Talked *all* the time. 'Always flappin' his mouth,' some said." Shooting, running, talking—it doesn't make any difference. The name fit and stuck.

If Flap Robertson was nervous about playing in the most important game in the history of Crispus Attucks, he did not show it. Through some error, his name had been left off the roster during the sectional tournament. As he later recalled, "When I got a chance to play in the regional, I wanted to make sure the coach would remember who I was." No sooner did he touch the ball than he shot it, a fifteen-foot jumper that cut the spread to eight points and, according to Jim Cummings, a writer for the

African American *Indianapolis Recorder*, "rekindled a spark of hope in Attucks hearts." His prose might have been a little heated and partisan, but Cummings was nonetheless accurate. "If sophomore Bailey Robertson—who didn't even play in the sectional games—could score so easily, so can we," seemed the sentiment of the older players.[2]

Willie Gardner—taller, thinner, poorer than most of the other kids on the team—made two quick baskets. The 6'8" Gardner had joined the team at midseason, and since then Attucks had not lost a game. And if he could help it, the Tigers would not lose this one. Bob Jewell, the Attucks player whom every parent held up as an example of how to behave, helped Gardner by making a free throw. In one minute and twenty-nine seconds the Anderson lead had shrunk to three points, 72-69. "I've never heard anything like it," commented a person who was at the game. It was almost as if the fifteen thousand people watching the game had been divided along racial lines as they entered the barnlike Butler Fieldhouse, whites going to the choice seats and blacks relegated to the area behind the Attucks bench and in the back bleachers, where all the police congregated. But as Crispus Attucks struggled to get back in the game, the black corner was alive with activity. Some people were crying, and a few had fainted. Anderson fans were also screaming, but a frantic note had replaced the smugness.

Sitting close to the floor, Crispus Attucks's principal, Russell Lane, and athletic director, Alonzo Watford, were as nervous as the other Tiger supporters. But they were less concerned about the game than the behavior of the team and fans. On the court the players raced about frantically, their desire and their passion palpable. In the Attucks stands spectators screamed their encouragement, loud, holding nothing back. Across the floor Anderson fans cheered just as zealously, adding a racial edge to their cries of support. "Shamefully partisan," *Indianapolis Star* sportswriter Bob Collins would later describe the behavior of the Anderson fans. In this atmosphere anything could—might— happen. A wild scramble for the ball. A heatedly contested call. A fight on the court. A brawl in the stands. Anything. Lane and Watford had labored to get their school included in the state tournament, giving their black players a chance to compete against the white players. They had not—definitely not—sought an emotional confrontation. They had not wanted this.[3]

But the game had leaped beyond them. Anderson pushed the ball up the court fast and out of control and turned it over. Gardner got the ball once again. He drove toward the basket, began to shoot, and was hacked. Clearly, as far as Attucks supporters were concerned, a two-shot foul. But the referee signaled that Gardner was not shooting. One shot. His free throw cut the Anderson lead to 72-70. No sooner had Anderson's J. D. Alder increased his team's margin to 74-70 than Attucks's Hallie Bryant reduced it to two again with a twisting turnaround shot. The Crispus Attucks corner exploded with noise, breaking into the "Crazy Song." The fans sang:

> *Oh, Anderson is rough*
> *And Anderson is tough*
> *They can beat everybody*
> *But they can't beat us*
> *Hi-de-hi-de, hi-de-hi*
> *Hi-de-hi-de, hi-de-ho*
> *That's the skip, bob, beat-um*
> *That's the crazy song.*

A referee's whistle cut into the celebration. A touch foul. Willie Gardner's fifth. He was out. Gardner, a future Harlem

Globetrotter, joined fellow starter John Davis on the bench. Anderson increased its lead to 75-72. Two minutes and thirty-eight seconds remained in the game.

But Attucks kept fighting, and it had the players to do it. As a result of the segregationist educational policies in Indianapolis, the school did not have to depend on one good player, or two, or three. The team was loaded. With Gardner out of the game, sophomore Hallie Bryant, another future Globetrotter, took over. He grabbed an inbounds pass, drove the length of the court, and scored. Then he helped force a turnover and made another twisting shot from the top of the key, giving Attucks a 76-75 lead. Bob Collins called Bryant's performance under extraordinary pressure "above words," and he characterized the entire game as a time when "the unusual became commonplace, the improbable easy."[4]

Gradually during the second half of the game the referees had been exerting more control. With alarming regularity they awarded two shots to Anderson for Attucks's fouls and one to Attucks for Anderson's fouls. Crispus Attucks head coach Ray Crowe and assistant coach Al Spurlock believed their players were capable of winning the game, but they were not sure the officials would allow them. After the game Spurlock admitted he was "kind'a scared because of the bad officiating," and years later he added, "By the end of the game it seemed as if Anderson had seven players on the court—two with striped uniforms."[5]

For a time the game became a free-throw contest. Anderson's high scorer, J. D. Alder, made two, giving his team a one-point lead. Attucks's Benny Cook missed two, but Jewell tipped in the second, taking the lead back. Next time up the court Cook was fouled again, making one of two this time. Crispus Attucks now led 79-77.

Benny Cook then turned from hackee to hacker. In quick succession he fouled Herb Hood and Jack Tilley. Hood made one of his two free throws; Tilley, pale and tired, made both of his. With twenty-three seconds remaining in the game, Anderson led 80-79.

In his mother's home, twelve-year-old Oscar Robertson watched the game, proud of the black athletes running up and down the court. He had heard of other great black athletes, mostly boxers like Joe Louis, Sugar Ray Robinson, and Kid Gavilan. He had even listened to their fights on the radio. But now the faces on television were familiar; one was Flap's, his brother's. Though this was the first Crispus Attucks game Oscar had ever seen, he immediately grasped its importance. This was "something"— something in a city, a land, that offered nothing to blacks. Except for school, there was little to which Oscar looked forward. Gangs, white and black, had kept him pinned in his west-side neighborhood; poverty and racism had barred him from most entertainment facilities. In a way that he did not fully understand at the time, the game on the television screen gave him hope.

Twenty-three seconds. Benny Cook and Flap Robertson brought the ball up the court against light defense. In front of the Attucks bench, coaches Crowe and Spurlock tried to get their players' and the referees' attention. They wanted a time-out, a chance to set up a play. Nobody, not the players, officials, or spectators, paid them the slightest attention. With twelve seconds left the ball was in the hands of Charlie West, a substitute forward who had made only one basket during the game but knew what it took to become a high school legend. He drove hard for the basket, pulled up, and attempted an acrobatic scoop shot. The ball fell short and set off a mad scramble that ended when Jack Tilley kicked it out-of-bounds. Attucks ball. Seven seconds.

Sitting high in the bleachers, Bailey Robertson Sr. observed the game with interest but without wild passion. In the din swirling around him, he was the quiet center. When a friend asked him why, all he said was, "There's ten boys out on that court. Five are going to win and five are going to lose." Sure he felt proud that his son was part of the action, but something in him already identified with the five who would lose.

Bob Jewell held up two fingers to set up an out-of-bounds play. He lifted the ball over his head. He did not intend to throw it to Flap Robertson, but Hallie Bryant was covered and Robertson was not. Flap caught the ball on the baseline far in the corner. Not looking for Bryant or anyone else, he jumped, cocked his wrist in his unusual style, and released it. "I just grabbed the ball, shot and prayed," he later told a reporter. Different people remembered the shot differently. Many recalled that it was a flat, archless shot that struck the side of the rim and bounded straight up. The ball kept climbing up and up, eight feet or more some would later say. Others, perhaps less inclined to poetic exaggeration, offered the opinion that the ball bounced only two or three feet above the rim. Coach Ray Crowe, however, insisted that the shot floated toward the basket with a lovely, high, glorious arch. In any case, it hung in the air above the rim long enough to seem like forever, a pregnant pause that delayed victory or defeat.[6]

On the court ten sets of players' eyes watched the ball. Two sets of officials' eyes watched the ball. Coaches, players on the bench, spectators in the stands, television viewers—they all watched the same ball. Oscar Robertson, sitting with his mother Mazell, watched.

It fell straight through the hoop. Crispus Attucks won 81-80 in what a deeply proud *Indianapolis Recorder* reporter called "without a doubt, one of the most thrilling high school basketball games ever played in Indiana—or the world." Sportswriter

Bob Collins was considerably less partisan but no less impressed, labeling the game "the most dramatic and exciting" in tournament history. Flap Robertson recalled, "Later people told me their relatives died of heart attacks. One lady said she started to go into labor when the ball went through."[7]

The black crowd in the corner erupted in a spontaneous celebration. But that outburst could not match the mood in west Indianapolis. As soon as the game ended the streets in the black section of the city bustled with activity. The heart of the street celebrations was Indiana Avenue, once the glittering center of Indianapolis African American nightlife. Indiana Avenue was still the hub, but much of the glitter was gone. But on this night no one noticed the decline. Traffic crawled up and down the Avenue, emitting horn blasts and cries of joy. "Ba-ad, ba-a-ad Tigers," smiling residents greeted one another, then talked about the game and the certainty of upcoming semifinal and state victories.

White Indianapolis authorities were not sure what to make of either the victory or the celebrations. Crispus Attucks was, after all, a local team, and few local teams had ever seemed as talented as the Tigers. But it was a local team without a white player, and the excitement along Indiana Avenue was vaguely disquieting, almost as if the servants had taken over the house for a party. Just to be on the safe side, Audry Jacobs, head of the police traffic division, sent extra patrolmen to the west side and toured the area himself.

An hour or so after the game ended Coach Crowe and his team arrived to take part in the festivities. They ate a late dinner of ham and sweet potatoes at Seldon's Cafe, stopping often to shake a hand or acknowledge a greeting. They were tired and very happy, and after dinner newspapers reported they walked to

Crispus Attucks for a bonfire and a snake dance. It was early in the morning by the time they began to float toward home.

Long before Flap arrived home, Oscar Robertson was in bed and asleep. But somehow his life would never be the same. His world, and the world of his black Indianapolis neighbors, had somehow, almost magically, expanded. Something different had happened, something that produced joy and hope. It was almost as if Joe Louis were a local fighter and had knocked out Max Schmeling in Indianapolis. And his brother Flap had played a key role in the event. The name—Robertson—had taken on new meaning for every person he knew. Basketball and joy, race and achievement, had begun to come together.

The game had odd powers. Like great art, it had the ability to transcend and transform reality. It could raise players and spectators above their sometimes squalid and mundane lives or torpedo them into abject depression, and in that sense it was always more than a game. It was the intersection of art and politics, community and finance—and this was evident in no year more than 1951. While the drama of the Crispus Attucks Tigers occupied center stage in Indiana, another, far darker performance was running its course in New York City. Like ill-matched teammates, beside the Crispus Attucks stories in the Indianapolis newspapers lurked the unfolding drama of the 1951 basketball scandals.

At the beginning of 1951 college basketball was king. The National Invitational Tournament attracted interest throughout the country, the National Collegiate Athletic Association tournament was growing in popularity, and conference races occupied the attention of millions of basketball fans during the long winter months. But with so much attention and such fanatical

supporters, the sport also gained a devoted following among organized and unorganized crime. The point spread seemed tai-
lored for basketball and its players. In theory—and often enough
in reality—a few talented players on a good team could control,
or at least influence, the margin of victory. They could play well
enough for their team to win but not well enough to beat the
point spread. It was a win-win proposition—win the game, win
the bets. And by 1951 every wise guy on the streets knew that
many of the best players in the country were active in both
pursuits.[8]

In early 1951 what was bound to happen did. The crime
of point shaving and game fixing found its way to the desk of
Manhattan district attorney Frank Hogan, a midlevel public ser-
vant with high-level ambitions. It was not the hardest criminal
nut to crack; most of the players who had accepted bribes were
decent-enough college kids who began blabbing and blubbering
as soon as they reached the inside of a police station, and often
even before. So many players were involved that Hogan's main
difficulty was choosing where to begin. For example, the City
College of New York, the 1950 NIT and NCAA champions, was
rich in fixers. At one time or another during the season all five
starters and the top two reserves had shaved points or fixed games.
At times different players blew shots, flubbed rebounds, and tossed
errant passes for different gambling syndicates, occasionally at
cross-purposes. Only the spread of the scandal deflected some of
the public attention away from CCNY. New York schools ab-
sorbed the most punishing blows. Serious problems surfaced at
Long Island University, New York University, Manhattan College, and Saint John's College, although Hogan, a good Catholic,
steered his investigation away from the latter school. But Hogan
also uncovered fixers at such leading midwestern universities as
Toledo, Bradley, and Kentucky.

Midwestern fish were the last Hogan trolled. While Crispus Attucks was competing in the Indiana high school championships it was still possible for midwesterners to believe that the fixes were a northeastern, urban problem, mainly confined to blacks, Jews, Italians, and other "shady types." "Out here in the Midwest these scandalous conditions, of course, do not exist," the sanctimonious University of Kansas coach Forrest "Phog" Allen told reporters. "But in the East, the boys, particularly those who participate in the resort hotel leagues during the summer months, are thrown into an environment which cannot help but breed the evil which more and more is coming to light." The equally self-righteous University of Kentucky coach Adolph Rupp agreed: "Gamblers couldn't get at my boys with a ten-foot pole." In short, midwesterners observed a clear difference between the ethnically diverse urban players and the wholesome, generally WASPish heartland athletes.[9]

Black and urban, Crispus Attucks, however, found itself outside the cozy parameters of midwestern sports. But its victory over Anderson brought it inside the tent, much to the discomfort of many Hoosiers. Although every now and then the name *Indianapolis* Crispus Attucks—a modifier never before attached to the school—appeared in a newspaper, most editors gave more space to Attucks's seemingly over-energetic victory celebrations. Cries of "ba-ad, ba-a-ad Tigers," long-lined snake dances, and meals of greens and sweet potato pie clued white Hoosiers everywhere that Crispus Attucks was a world apart from Anderson.[10]

But the school had a spot in the semifinals the following Saturday, and Anderson did not. Not since 1945 had an Indianapolis team made it to the state finals. With two victories at the semifinal tournament in Butler Fieldhouse, Crispus Attucks could end that unseemly embarrassment. The Tigers accomplished both with remarkable ease. In the afternoon game they played

Covington, whose coach promised that his team would control "the two big boys" (Bob Jewell and Willie Gardner) and contain the Crispus Attucks fast break. Once the game began, Covington players promptly ignored their coach and lost by forty points, the biggest spread since 1916. The evening contest was not much tighter. Attucks swept past Batesville 62-42, making it only the fourth city school to reach the final four.[11]

Once again black residents of Indianapolis celebrated. Along Indiana Avenue Attucks faithful expressed their certainty that their team would capture the state title the following week: "It's in the bag." "The cup is ours." Once again the team ate a late dinner at Seldon's Cafe, and a victory bonfire burned early into the morning. But school officials celebrated in a subdued manner, voicing pride but nothing even approaching overconfidence. Alonzo Watford spoke of the quality of the next opponent and the need for continued sportsmanship, not the margin of the recent victories.[12]

During the next week talk of race and basketball mixed uneasily in the newspapers, streets, and offices of Indianapolis, creating official and unofficial subtexts. The official line was that race did not matter. The *Indianapolis Recorder* was so insistent on this point that any reader might wonder if, in fact, race was unimportant why it had to be mentioned so often. In one article, a *Recorder* writer observed that the Tigers would play in the state tournament "not alone for their school . . . but for the honor of their city and the pride of their fellow townsmen." White and black Indianapolis residents, he claimed, supported Crispus Attucks. An ugly incident in the Attucks-Batesville game demonstrated the town's solidarity. Early in the contest a white drunk bellowed out, "Stop the niggers! I'm for the whites—I'm always for the whites!" And when several young white girls sitting close to him began cheering for Crispus Attucks, he told them, "Now you girls can all go down on the Avenue and get raped." At that point a white man turned around, angrily saying, "Listen, mister. I am from Indianapolis, and that team out there is our Indianapolis team! That color talk of yours doesn't enter into it." Another white man added, "And that goes for me, too."[13]

But submerged even in these denials that race mattered was the message that sport was the reason for the unexpected harmony. "Many a white has put the Satan of race prejudice behind him and jumped wholeheartedly on the Attucks bandwagon," observed an editorialist. "All this is eminently to the good. Our city has needed something like this, to erase the hostility built up by race-mongering. . . . It is cheering to discover that old Naptown has a heart after all, and that the spark of humanity still resides in the breast of the average Hoosier. Where the appeals of religion, reason and education seem to have fallen on deaf ears, the spectacle of brilliant basketball has turned the trick. In deep humility we observe that God does move in mysterious ways."[14]

Not everyone, of course, followed the official line. Many Attucks supporters argued that race was important and that it did matter. They pointed to the close calls that always seemed to go against their school. Race mattered to the referees. They decried the health of a city where Hallie Bryant, Willie Gardner, and John Davis were cheered on the basketball court but could not find decent summer jobs, move freely about their city, or eat in restaurants where their exploits provided dinner conversation. In all significant ways, race still mattered.[15]

Willie Gardner recalled the mood of the times: "We were a group of fifteen and sixteen-year-old kids who were just as tickled about winning as any group would have been and I'm sure that was the same case for our fans. But the larger community thought we were animals or something. I have no idea what would make them think that way. We were taught from day one that if we ever did anything stupid, then the whole school and community would suffer. That stuff didn't bother us. We'd come to expect it. But, as I got older, I wondered what ever made those people think we were interested in destroying our own community and school."[16]

The reality of life in Indianapolis gave rise to the unofficial line: race relations would be damaged if Crispus Attucks won the state crown. This was the subtlest of messages, undocumented by newspaper articles or official memorandums. It was simply a feeling, passed down from the city fathers to Principal Russell Lane to Coach Crowe and his players. There was no talk of intentionally losing—this was not a point-shaving scandal—just instructions not to press so hard and to be good sportsmen above all else. Throughout the tournament Lane had attended practices, addressing players as a team and talking to them in private, reminding them to play hard but play clean.

Shortly before Crispus Attucks's afternoon game with Evansville Reitz in the state tournament, Lane once again spoke with Crowe's team. Cheering pierced the walls of the locker room. The players were preparing for the game, thinking only about winning. Lane gave them something else to consider. Short and simple: "You are representing much more than your school. . . . You *are* black Indianapolis. This time, the whole state is watching. More important than winning is that you demonstrate good sportsmanship. Be gentlemen." Willie Gardner tuned Lane out. Bob Jewell, a product of a middle-class family from the more affluent north side—a student-council president who had played Dr. Lane on Student Day—listened. He had never fouled out of a game. He was a gentleman. He would play like one.[17]

The game began like a hundred-yard dash. Conventional wisdom held that the only way to defeat Crispus Attucks was to play a slow, controlled game. The Reitz players did the opposite. They ran and shot, repeatedly taking advantage of Attucks's soft zone and man-to-man defenses. They also were more concerned with winning than sportsmanship, and according to one reporter "used a little more muscle and were a little less clean than the Tigers." Reitz's center, Jerry Whitesell, dined on Jewell's generous gentlemanly defense, leading his team with nineteen points. Adding to Attucks's problems, consistently throughout the game close calls and "questionable calls" went in Reitz's favor. Whenever Attucks took or threatened to take the lead its players were whistled for fouls. For instance, toward the end of the third quarter, with Attucks leading 46-45, a Reitz player grabbed a rebound under the Tigers' basket but came down out-of-bounds. As the clock continued to tick, the referees conferred, finally handing the ball to Reitz. Although Attucks crept within one point of Reitz late in the fourth quarter—when another call went against the Tigers—the Evansville school won the game 66-59.[18]

In defeat Attucks supporters sought consolation. If their team had not played particularly well, it had played cleanly. Jewell might have been outplayed, but he had not been "out-gentlemanned." He won the coveted Arthur L. Trester Award—named after a man who had struggled long and hard to keep black teams out of the state championships—for the player who best exemplifies "the ideal of the scholar-athlete-citizen." Years later Jewell still remembered the empty feeling. Being a gentleman was still important, but losing in the state finals hurt badly. "It was a Band-aid on a gaping wound," he said of the Trester Award.[19]

If the Crispus Attucks run in 1951 had not ended with a state title, it had raised the possibility, so long submerged in the Indianapolis black community, of success—complete, uplifting, seldom-even-considered, beautiful success. Victory. Someday.

After the run Oscar Robertson became consumed by the game. That Christmas he got an orange ball. He dribbled it to school. He played on the local courts after classes and at the YMCA when the wind and snow drove the players inside. He asked Willie Gardner and Hallie Bryant and his brother Flap how they did certain things. They talked, he listened. They taught, he learned. And he practiced and played, played and practiced.

Chapter One

BAILEY'S SON

Bailey Robertson Sr. claimed that his grandfather lived in the South for 116 years. Born in 1838, two years after Davy Crockett died at the Alamo, Marshall Collier had been sold on the auction block, experienced the joy of emancipation, suffered the disillusionment of "race adjustment," and kept planting and harvesting crops until his eyesight failed and he was too old to do much of anything useful. But even in his last years this tall (some said he was over seven feet), erect man remained inordinately proud, if a bit short with his grandchildren and great-grandchildren. Then he fell down some steps he had no business being on, broke a hip, and never recovered. He never left Tennessee. Saw no reason to. And his son felt the same way, although he did not live half as long. He died in 1923, the same year as President Warren G. Harding—though with considerably less fanfare—leaving two young sons behind.[1]

Bailey Robertson did not share his father and grandfather's complacency. It was not that he hated the South or had an itch to roam; nor was it a matter of finding work or escaping responsibilities. He was attached to the corn and cotton land around Bellsburg, Tennessee, by friends and family, work and community. "I worked for a white guy who treated me well," he remembered. He made eight to twelve dollars a week, a considerable increase from the fifty cents a day he made during "Hoover's time." But it wasn't the money, it was the changing "times"—or, perhaps more precisely, the fact that times were not changing in Dickson County, Tennessee.

Bailey had three young sons—Bailey Jr., Oscar, and Henry—and he could see pretty clearly the arch of their lives if they remained in Tennessee. He had finished sixth grade before he left school to work full time. Probably his sons would get that far. But what then? There were no white high schools around that admitted black children, and there were no black high schools close enough for them to attend. They could not get a "proper education" in the South, and if they could not get a proper education, what chance had they to do better than he? As his eldest son moved toward his last years of elementary school, Bailey sensed that he was reaching a decisive moment.

Mazell Bell Robertson, Bailey's wife, agreed. Like her husband, she had been reared in Dickson County, near the Mount Zion African Methodist Episcopal Church. In that part of Dickson County, everyone, black and white alike, admired her parents, Early and Pearly Bell. People addressed them as Uncle Early and Aunt Pearly out of respect, which they had earned through a lifetime of hard work and clean living. Early believed strongly in self-sufficiency. He had worked on the Ohio River to earn the money to buy his own land; then he dug his own 187-foot well, worked his own mules, and milked his own cow. During the day he grew corn, black-eyed peas, hay, and tobacco on his own land, and he worked twenty acres of Cumberland River bottomland for a white man named Lightfoot. His son Russell remembered that he left the house before sunrise and returned after dark, but even then there was more work to do. At night he sat on his porch shelling peas and singing hymns, his favorite being "Love Lifted Me," which he sang loudly and with passion. But he probably knew that what had worked for him might not be enough for his grandchildren. He stressed the need for education, and he saw that the nature of agriculture in the South was changing. Tractors and harvesters were replacing mules and small farmers. And where was a black man supposed to get the money to purchase expensive farm machinery? A bank? That was an idea that drew more than one smile in Dickson County. No, Early believed, and so did his wife and daughter, that his grandchildren needed more opportunities than his small Tennessee world had to offer.

A larger world was not unknown to the Bells and the Robertsons. In the North, in Indianapolis, Indiana, Bailey Sr. had an aunt who had encouraged him to move his family there. During World War II he had spent some months in Indianapolis working in a defense plant, but lonely without Mazell and the kids, his stay had been brief. Maybe he thought of returning someday with his family; maybe he didn't. Half a century later he had forgotten. But if the earlier experience did not hatch a thought, it planted a seed of a thought. The thought was an outgrowth of the African American dream—a vision of a better life up north.

It was the great dream of Bailey's generation. For many blacks the South held little, save bitter memories of backbreaking labor and exploitation. "These Mississippi towns ain't/ Fit fer a hoppin' toad," poet Langston Hughes wrote in "Bound No'th Blues." Throughout the South a story had been told. After a year of hard work a black tenant farmer took his cotton crop to his white boss. The boss weighed and calculated, scratching his head and jotting down figures. Then he announced that the tenant's five bales of cotton exactly balanced his debt. The black farmer smiled, saying that he had another bale outside. The bale, he reasoned, would give him a little economic breathing room. "Shucks," complained the boss, "why didn't you tell me before? Now I'll have to figure the account all over again to make it come out even."[2]

Maybe the story was true. Perhaps it wasn't. But it did illustrate a larger truth for Bailey and Mazell's generation. Although slavery belonged to the distant past, freedom in the South was still too much of a legal abstraction. Tenant farmers and share-croppers lived in a perpetual cycle of debt, borrowing money and tools throughout the year and always coming up a tad short at the end of it. And even for men like Early, who owned and worked their own land, economic disaster was always a cold, haunting possibility. Low agricultural prices and high interest rates guaranteed season after season of increasing debt, and if by chance a harvest was bountiful or some international crisis forced up prices, white landowners could always juggle the figures to the tenant's disadvantage, or white store owners could always raise their prices. Harsh living conditions only made things worse. Flimsy wooden shacks and wood-burning stoves were no match for chilly winter winds, and indoor plumbing was rare.[3]

A violent social system and an unjust political system added to the misery created by the exploitative economic system. By the time Early Bell was born in 1882, the process of forced segregation in public facilities, restriction of voting rights, and limitation of job opportunities for African Americans was well under way. *Plessy v. Ferguson* (1896), the Supreme Court case that sanctioned the doctrine of "separate but equal" and enshrined the notion of a Jim Crow world, only legitimized what had already taken place. Blacks were separate but far from equal. State and local governments underfunded their schools, paid little attention to their facilities, and treated them like permanent second-class citizens. White town councils established curfews for blacks but not whites. Black deliverymen always entered a white man's house through the back door, and black cooks ate their meals on the back porch. If they were to maintain their economic and social status, southern whites needed docile and respectful black workers. Any violation of this social code met with swift, furious "justice." Standing up to a white man, using a white facility, or—worst of all—flirting with a white woman were grounds for a beating or lynching. While "uppity" blacks were hanged and burned for various social transgressions, local governments and law enforcement turned a blind eye. Preserving the code of supremacy was all that mattered. Blacks privately raged but also gulped in fear, afraid they might be next.

If the humiliation, despair, and terror of southern life were not enough, two crises helped push southern blacks off the land and toward northern cities. In the late nineteenth century, Mississippi valley floods periodically overwhelmed flimsy levees. And by the turn of the century, the nefarious boll weevil infiltrated large portions of the southern cotton belt. Feeding solely on the cotton boll, the tiny insect destroyed up to 50 percent of the cotton crop in some regions, limiting planter profits and the extension of credit to black tenants. Increasingly, blacks had enough. Entrenched in a racist and violent social system, and without economic prospects, their eyes turned north.[4]

During World War I, northern industrial cities increasingly welcomed black migrants from the South. At a time when the huge flow of European immigrants slowed to a trickle, American industries needed a large labor force to supply munitions and other war-related materials. Blacks answered the call, buoyed by the prospect of high wages, better schools, political rights, and exciting urban life. Migrants sang, "Bound for the Promised

Land." Special trains carrying workers to northern cities bore slogans etched in chalk: "Farewell—We're Good and Gone" and "Bound to the Land of Hope." Between 1910 and 1920 the number of blacks entering northern states roughly tripled from the previous decade, and between 1920 and 1930 the figure doubled again. The vibrant economy and budding consumer culture of the Roaring Twenties fed a growing demand for industrial jobs. From New York's Harlem to Chicago's South Side, black "ghettos" housed black businesses and cultural institutions. Poverty and discrimination did not disappear, but northern cities at least held the hope of a better life. The sociologist E. Franklin Frazier reported that as some trains crossed the Ohio River, "the migrants signalized the event by kissing the ground and holding prayer services."[5]

Word spread throughout the South, reaching even to remote rural areas such as Bellsburg, Tennessee. Northern industries hired white labor agents and black preachers to tour southern states, exhorting people to come north. Black newspapers such as the *Chicago Defender* spread the word, advertising not only jobs but the legal benefits of citizenship. Black southerners listened, hearing how friends and relatives prospered in the cities, voted in elections, sat in the front of the bus. Many returned south for brief stretches, driving fancy cars and exhibiting a new brashness in front of whites. Local police called it the "Attitude," and they didn't like it. A black man visiting home was liable to get the windows of his new car smashed in. He was in the South, after all, a land where old rules died hard. The region was filled with tension over the ultimate impact of the migration north. The *Georgia Enquirer Sun* worried over the mass exodus, noting that "our plantations are large, our climate is peculiar, and we ourselves are not accustomed to doing the work that we ask the negro to do." Others thought of the problems in store for northern cities; the *Vicksburg Herald* proclaimed that "wherever there is a negro infusion, there will be a race problem—a white man's burden—which they are destined to share."[6]

The *Herald* made a valuable point. The Great Migration made race relations a national rather than a regional issue. Crowded, segregated housing and persistent discrimination faced the new migrants. In 1919 a rash of race riots broke out in northern cities. Yet even though racial tensions continued to smolder in the ensuing decades, the movement north continued. Although job prospects virtually disappeared during the Great Depression of the 1930s, a substantial migration persisted, testifying to the brutal conditions in the South. By the 1940s the exodus once again intensified. The widespread commercial use of the mechanical cotton picker solved the labor demands of white farmers and rendered black tenant farmers and sharecroppers expendable. Even more important, World War II led to a new surge in demand for black labor. Between 1940 and 1944 the number of black workers in wartime industries such as steel, machinery, aircraft, and shipbuilding tripled. The increasing necessity of black labor allowed for significant political breakthroughs. Labor leader A. Philip Randolph threatened to mount a protest rally in Washington, D.C., in 1941, leading the Roosevelt administration to issue an executive order barring discrimination in defense industries and creating a Fair Employment Practices Commission.[7]

These conditions of war and labor demands, discrimination and hope for a better life, were part of the air Bailey Robertson Sr. breathed. If they did not dictate his move north, they shaped his thinking and influenced his options. Had he had family in New York City, Chicago, Detroit, Cleveland, or Philadelphia, he probably would have moved to one of those cities. But he had family in Indianapolis, and that made all the difference.

"Ain't God good to Indiana?" asked the poet William Herschell in 1919. Most Hoosiers would have nodded yes. No other state could provide that "snug-up feelin' like a mother gives a child" in quite the same fashion. Hoosiers cherished the notion that they represented not only what was typical, but also what was the best about America. They were white. They were Protestant. They farmed. Enough said. The writer Irvin S. Cobb explained in 1924 that the Hoosier character was rooted in "old-fashioned philosophies springing out of the soil and smelling of the pennyrile and the sassafrack." These traditions included "old-fashioned cookery, old-fashioned decencies, old-fashioned virtues," and, Cobb added, "old-fashioned bigotries."[8]

Even in Indianapolis this comfortable myth endured. Attracted by jobs in the automobile industry and wartime manufacturing, small-town Hoosiers invaded the capital in the early twentieth century. The city billed itself as the "Crossroads of America" and the "Capital of the Land of Opportunity." The population tripled between 1890 and 1920, even as the percentage of foreign born shrank due to stricter immigration laws and World War I, allowing locals to praise "this 100 percent American town." The ethnic groups that remained were subject to heavy doses of small-town xenophobia. City officials banned German language courses from the school curriculum in 1918. More significantly, at least 25 percent of eligible Indianapolitans joined the Ku Klux Klan, which dominated state politics in the 1920s. Spouting anti-Catholic and anti-Jewish rhetoric, the Klan rose to power on the idea that it represented rural, populist values in an era of encroaching urbanization and ethnic diversity.[9]

White Hoosiers' enmity steadily came to focus on blacks as well. As the immigrant population declined, the African American population surged. By 1930 almost 44,000 blacks lived in Indianapolis, over 12 percent of the city's population. Some two-thirds of the state's black population was born outside of Indiana, mostly in Kentucky and Tennessee. In Indianapolis the influx strained the housing situation in black neighborhoods, and the more established black families began looking for homes in white, middle-class neighborhoods. With the clash of populations came an end to the idea of down-home harmony. White home owners who feared declines in real-estate values and encroachment of unwanted "coloreds" formed civic leagues to persuade other whites from selling or leasing property to blacks. One such league isolated and antagonized blacks by building "spite fences" around their properties, and in at least one neighborhood, league members circulated handbills asking, "DO YOU WANT A NIGGER FOR A NEIGHBOR?"[10]

Soon the city government got in the act. Urged on by a group calling itself the White Citizens Protective League, Indianapolis's city council in 1926 enacted a residential zoning ordinance segregating black and white neighborhoods. It specified that one could not take up residence in a neighborhood of the "opposite" race without the written consent of the majority of people in that neighborhood. Outraged blacks, led by the local branch of the National Association for the Advancement of Colored People, organized a test case. An Indianapolis judge found the ordinance in violation of citizens' constitutional rights, a decision that was reinforced by a subsequent United States Supreme Court decision on a similar ordinance in New Orleans. Thwarted in their attempt to institutionalize residential segregation, white Indianapolitans turned to more subtle measures. White realtors refused to sell white property to interested blacks, and some home owners signed covenants pledging not to sell to non-Caucasians. Blacks may have invaded Indianapolis, many whites thought, but they could still be kept separated from white neighborhoods, white businesses, and white institutions.[11]

White hostility was hardly a new phenomenon for blacks, and they did what they had done in the past—turn inward, developing their own neighborhoods, their own businesses, and their own institutions. The local branch of the YMCA on Senate Avenue had the largest membership of any black YMCA in the country. In addition to religious and recreational programs, the Senate Avenue YMCA also hosted cultural programs, including an annual series of public lectures called "Monster Meetings," which featured such speakers as W. E. B. Du Bois, Paul Robeson, Eleanor Roosevelt, Adam Clayton Powell Jr., and Thurgood Marshall. Businesses also thrived. Madam C. J. Walker, reportedly the first black woman millionaire in the United States, moved her business to Indianapolis in 1910. A leader in the black business community, she was also a philanthropist. Originally marketing hair-care products, Walker built an empire that included more than twenty thousand employees. Her famed Walker Building, built in 1927, included a casino, beauty college, drugstore, coffee shop, and business offices, and it hosted films and vaudeville shows.[12]

Walker's was just one of many independent businesses that thrived along Indiana Avenue, the commercial and cultural center of black Indianapolis in the first half of the twentieth century. As early as 1916 the district housed 142 residential units, 33 restaurants, 33 saloons, 26 grocery stores, 17 barbershops and hairstylists, 16 tailors and clothing stores, 14 shoemakers, 13 dry goods stores, some undertakers, a bicycle repair shop, a hotel, and a medical facility. Fire and police stations staffed with blacks preserved order and developed an even greater autonomy from white authority. And as the black population grew, politicians recognized black voters as a political force. During Prohibition, in exchange for votes, officials rarely raided the soda counters, restaurants, pool halls, and barbershops where bootlegged liquor flowed freely.[13]

During the 1920s Indiana Avenue boomed. It was an African American mecca, similar to Harlem in New York City, Beale Street in Memphis, Walnut Street in Louisville, or Twelfth and Vine in Kansas City, one of the very few places in America that was so black and so alive that it glowed with its own peculiar sense of hope. One resident recalled, "You could walk through the Avenue and get anything you wanted. Friendship . . . entertainment . . . anything. There were people everywhere, all along the sidewalks and even in the street. You could go there at three on a Saturday afternoon, stay there until two Sunday morning, and have a real blast."[14]

The prosperity of the twenties screeched to a halt with the onset of the Great Depression. Historian Emma Lou Thornbrough called the decade "a disaster of unparalleled proportions" for Indiana blacks, as unemployed whites displaced blacks from menial jobs they would have rejected during better times. New Deal programs provided relief for limited numbers, but trade unions protested any allotment of skilled work to black laborers under the Works Progress Administration. During the construction of Lockefield Gardens, a successful federally funded housing project for blacks, African Americans worked only in unskilled, lower-paying jobs. But the opening of Lockefield Gardens in 1938 at least gave many blacks affordable quality housing and a sense of community.[15]

The economic troubles of the 1930s and the need to attract consumer dollars spurred a gradual change in the character of Indiana Avenue. Many residents vacated their homes, some businesses closed, and the focus shifted to providing food and entertainment. Restaurants included Porter Jones's barbecue stand, Joyner's Chili Parlor, and Ma Smothers's Eatery, where a customer could buy anything from chitterlings to pumpkin pie. After eating, a person could scan the latest releases at Kid Edwards's Record

Shop or grab a coffee at Brown's Beanery. Palmer Richardson's P&P Club even had a miniature golf course. Even more visibly, lounges and clubs opened along the Avenue.[16]

Into the 1940s the strip picked up nicknames such as "Funky Broadway," the "Yellow Brick Road," and the "Grand Ol' Street." The Sunset Terrace, the Cotton Club, the Trianon Ballroom, the Rainbow Palm Gardens, and Danny's Dreamland hosted famous entertainers such as Count Basie, Sarah Vaughan, Cab Calloway, and Josephine Baker. The Hamptons, a family of jazz musicians, settled in Indianapolis in the 1930s and developed into a well-known swing band. Nationally recognized musicians such as Wes Montgomery, J. J. Johnson, and Freddie Hubbard helped develop the unique "Indy Sound." Indiana Avenue was the center of black entertainment, and not just for blacks; some popular clubs regularly served an integrated clientele.[17]

The good times would not last. By the 1950s the character of the street was changing. By the end of the decade the Avenue had lost much of its glitter and had become a center for prostitution, gambling, and low-life saloons. The few remaining clubs occasionally hosted one-night stands by local musicians, but the glamorous era was gone. With the decline of Indiana Avenue came the physical deterioration of the entire neighborhood. Businesses were boarded and houses deserted. Ironically, the Avenue's dilapidation occurred as new economic opportunities arose for the growing black population. World War II had prompted a shortage in labor, and blacks answered the call. Their efforts were aided by federal policies that included the creation of the Fair Employment Practices Commission and the requirement of nondiscrimination for labor on war contracts. Labor unions increasingly accepted black workers, and the state passed a Fair Employment Practices Act. The wave of southern migrants became a flood. Between 1940 and 1950 the black population in

Indianapolis grew twice as quickly as the general population. Between 1950 and 1960 the black population grew five times as fast. By 1960 one in five Indianapolis residents was black.[18]

When Bailey Robertson arrived in Indianapolis, Indiana Avenue was just beginning its long, slow decline, taking with it much of the vitality of the African American neighborhood. Not that the area had ever been Indianapolis's most desirable place to live. The west-side ghetto was surrounded by water—the Central Canal on the east, the White River on the south and west, and Fall Creek on the north. It was a low-lying area, prone to flooding, nasty smells, and disease. With a few exceptions, it was an area of narrow, crowded streets and alleys, some oiled dirt, others poorly maintained.

But as long as it remained a classic African American ghetto, where poor, middle-class, and wealthier blacks were forced to live, it was not uniformly bleak. The most affluent lived along California Street. "The black bourgeoisie," Bill Scott called them. Mostly born in Indianapolis, they owned the neighborhood businesses and formed the heart of the black middle class. The poorest lived along the canal in a section known as Frog Island, where dirt streets were the norm and indoor facilities uncommon. Bailey Robertson Sr. settled his family closer to Frog Island than California Street. The four-room shotgun house he purchased at 1005 Colton Street was close to Fall Creek in a section where the word "street" was singularly honorific. But it was no worse than what he had left in Tennessee, and inadequate housing and poverty were no disgrace. All it meant was that one family was no worse off than the next. "Let me tell you about being poor," Oscar Robertson would later recall. "If you didn't know anything better, you didn't miss it. We had a roof over our heads. We had enough to eat. We were happy."

Both parents worked to ensure their boys had the necessities. Bailey labored in a defense plant during the war then got a job cutting meat at Kingan and Company, a meat-packing plant on the White River. Mazell worked as a domestic and cook and later as a beautician. Both were loving, devoted parents. A boyhood friend of Oscar remembered that Bailey was a quiet man but the kind of father who rolled on the ground and played with his sons, that Mazell was something of the neighborhood mother, quick with a home-cooked meal and an opinion.

Oscar and the friends he grew up with remembered their world as one of extremes. At one pole was their neighborhood, a place of safety and stability. "Everyone cared about everyone else," Bill Swatts remembered. There was no need to lock doors, and parents watched out for all the neighborhood kids. "Respect and rules were important," said Swatts. "We respected our elders, respected figures of authority, did as we were told. If you didn't, your parents would set you straight." In the neighborhood not only parents instructed children. Oscar remembered, "The older guys taught the younger kids how to take care of themselves—taught you about games, what side of town to go on and what to do when you're out, and what to look for. Some taught you to fight. Some taught you to play basketball. Some taught you about situations with other people. They taught you how to take care of yourself."

Outside of the neighborhood was the other pole, a place of real and potential danger. "We did not go on the south side because it was all white," Oscar said. "The east side was very, very tough. We also did not go downtown. We weren't wanted there, and we didn't have any money to spend anyway. Some blacks lived on the north side, but we didn't have the means—the transportation means or the financial means—to go there. So we stayed close to home with the people we knew." In fact,

Oscar's world was even smaller than the west side. He and his friends avoided Indiana Avenue, which by the early 1950s had turned seedy. The two major theaters, the Lido and the Walker, were out-of-bounds for most of the youths. "All the crazies, the wild ones and the toughs went to the Lido," Swatts recalled. Oscar agreed, "The Lido was a dangerous place." The Walker was also rough—and snobbish. "Young people had to go upstairs," Oscar said. "The security was not that good, so it was loud and sort of crazy. We just didn't go."

He and his friends just didn't go to a lot of places. Douglass Park had the only African American swimming pool, but it was also a place where fights were common. Riverside Amusement Park, located on the northern edge of the African American neighborhood, had large roller coasters, a roller-skating rink, and scores of "whites only" signs. Only on designated "Colored Frolic Days" was the park opened to the black children who lived just outside its gates. But even on those days Oscar and his friends usually elected to stay closer to home.

As Oscar grew older his life began to narrow even more. The success of the Crispus Attucks Tigers in the 1951 tournament ignited a passion for basketball in the community. Here was something that the poorest of the poor, the most recent migrants from Mississippi, Alabama, and Tennessee, the west siders who lived on oiled streets in homes without running water, could excel in. It didn't take money or connections, only time and skill. On the west side the game consumed hundreds of kids like Oscar. They practiced and practiced, hoping to get into a game at the Dust Bowl at Lockefield Gardens or at the Senate Avenue YMCA. Probably no one practiced as much as Oscar. Even as a youth he studied the game, practicing moves by himself and accepting pointers from such players as Hallie Bryant and Willie Gardner.

And he got better and better. Friends remembered that each summer he would disappear to Tennessee for a few months to visit his family, only to return a little bigger and a little better, as if he were going to basketball camp rather than to work on his grandfather's farm. He was better than any kid his own age. The best seventh grader, the best eighth grader, the best ninth grader. The best shooter. The best passer. With the best court sense. He had a gift. He had the desire. And he loved to play, never really thinking about how good he was. "I just liked to play," he remembered. "I never thought about being better than anyone else." The game helped sustain him and give him a sense of identity. It was there to comfort him when his parents divorced. It made him stand out in his neighborhood. "Oscar Robertson," Edgar Searcy remembered, "was special. I knew it the first time I saw him dribbling a basketball." Coaches felt the same way. They watched and waited for him to reach Crispus Attucks.

Chapter Two

"The Awfulest Thing That Ever Happened"

Tennessee in the summer of 1953 had been much the same as in previous years, a mixed bag of work and joy, sweat and laughter. Oscar knew the routine. Almost as soon as he got off the bus in Nashville, he commenced visiting relatives. He made his rounds on foot, along lengthy dirt roads and well-beaten paths that rose and fell across the hot, rolling land. Aunts, uncles, cousins, half cousins, grandparents, great-grandparents, great-great-grandparents—his grandmother Pearly Bell insisted that he see everyone as soon as humanly possible.

His grandfather Early Bell was just as insistent that he start working when the sun rose on his first day after he arrived. By the time Oscar was in his teens it was assumed he could put in a "man's day" in the field. He picked tobacco, milked the cows, and did the other chores that needed to be done around a farm. Years later he still remembered the hard work of haying. "The wagon crawled along at two or three miles an hour, but sometimes it seemed like it was going forty or fifty miles an hour," Oscar said. "As it went along we had to pick up, throw, and stack the bales. You get strong doing that stuff." But at the time he was not overly conscious of how hard he was working. "Everyone worked long hours," he noted. "And, you know, they didn't complain. That's just the way it was, and no one questioned it or thought about it. At least I didn't."

Snakes were a different matter. Oscar was aware of them. There were water snakes in the bottomland, rattlesnakes wedged between rocks in the wooded areas, copperheads about anywhere, especially in the shade under bushes and tobacco plants. Stripping suckers from the plants, Oscar got to where he could sense a lurking copperhead. "People might think I'm crazy, but I could smell them," he said. "They smelled like cucumbers. Every time I smelled cucumbers, sure enough, there was a copperhead." There was even a big rat snake in the barn, which he could not smell. Many times when he was working in the loft he would suddenly find himself within striking distance of the snake, jump back, and let out an explosion of surprise. "Don't kill that snake," Early Bell would call out. "That's a good snake."

That was the rule of thumb in rural Dickson County. Let the good snakes alone and keep a mean snake dog around for the rest. And his grandfather had one of the meanest. The dog spent most of its time in the crawl space under Early's house, and seldom was it ever given anything to eat. When Oscar asked why, his grandfather replied, "I don't want that dog to depend on me. I might not always be around." Instead of waiting for table scraps, the dog adapted to its laissez-faire existence by foraging for itself, killing what it could and dragging it back under the house to eat. If Oscar attempted to befriend the animal, his efforts would be rewarded with a snarl and show of teeth. "Leave that dog alone," Early would instruct him.

Oscar liked Tennessee, especially on Sundays when his extended family would gather for church and reunions. He recalled that all the women went to the Mount Zion AME service, where a preacher with a big rolling voice would get the spirit bouncing off the walls. Many of the men stayed outside, took a sip or two of whiskey, talked about just about everything, and laughed a great deal. He had two cousins who were particularly good with their fists, and he liked to watch them "take care of themselves." They did not fight because they were angry, but because it gave them pleasure.

For Oscar the pattern of work, worship, and family gatherings was all part of the fabric of Tennessee life, seemingly timeless. The only dramatic change was in Oscar himself. Before he left for Tennessee he had begun a growth spurt. At the end of his freshman season he stood about five feet, eight inches tall, thin, looking younger than he was. By the time of tryouts his sophomore year he was a shade under six feet, two inches, still very young looking but strong from farmwork. The added inches were not offset by any lankiness, and playing basketball before the season his friends had noticed that Oscar's game had taken another leap forward. No longer was he just Flap's kid brother. Now he was a player with a game, capable of taking on Hallie Bryant or Flap and holding his own.

In fact, on the first day of tryouts, one friend encouraged him to take an audacious step. Following well-established procedures, before practice the players divided into two groups on the basketball court at Attucks. The first group was older and taller players, juniors and seniors trying out for the varsity. The other group was younger and smaller players, sophomores mostly, with a few juniors who had been cut the year before. Their goal was a position on the junior varsity team.

Oscar sat with the other sophomores, but glancing to his right he saw Bill Mason gesturing to him. "Come on over here," he motioned. It had not occurred to Oscar to attempt to make the varsity squad. A sophomore trying out for the varsity was almost unheard of, and Coach Ray Crowe had given Oscar no indication that he wanted the youngster on "his team." But on a whim, Oscar decided to give it a try. "To this day I don't know why," he said years later. "The varsity was almost a set team, but I went over anyway." On the junior varsity team he would have been the star. The varsity was a different matter. With no encouragement from the coach, with the reputation of his brother preceding him, with the other players looking doubtfully in his direction—he best have something to offer. The pressure was on.

But he was sitting in a school that had always shouldered an extra burden of pressure.

Members of the school board had decided to call it Thomas Jefferson High School, but naming an all-black high school after a famous white slave owner just struck some people as unseemly. Eventually the board bowed to the pressure from the city's African American community to change the name, but that was its only concession. It remained firm in its belief that black and white children should not learn to read and write or add and subtract together.

The story of Crispus Attucks High School began in the early 1920s at a moment when white Indianapolis was awkwardly attempting to adjust to multiple changes. City leaders welcomed some of the changes, especially the prosperity bred by the stockyards, railroads, and industries. Indianapolis novelist Booth Tarkington in *The Magnificent Ambersons* caught this energy for and worship of commercial growth: "The idealists . . . had one supreme theory: that the perfect beauty and happiness of cities and of human life was to be brought about by more factories; they had a mania for factories; there was nothing they would not do to cajole a factory away from another city; and they were never more piteously embittered than when another city cajoled one away from them."[1]

They greeted other changes less warmly. The migration of African Americans from the rural South and the waves of immigrants from southern and eastern Europe left many WASPish residents vaguely uncomfortable. The wealthiest business leaders, insulated in the finest neighborhoods, regarded the migrants and immigrants as a deep pool of cheap labor. Less affluent whites viewed the new arrivals as threats, rivals for semiskilled jobs and inexpensive houses. But the racist and nativist rhetoric of the Ku Klux Klan won followers in both groups.

The voice of the Klan in Indiana during the early 1920s was David C. Stephenson, a round-faced, weak-chinned son of a Texas sharecropper who, by his own admission, was "a nobody from nowhere." Stephenson seldom discussed the details of his early life, and when he did he usually lied, but in 1920 he showed up in Evansville, Indiana, and began to carve out a name for himself. The same year Stephenson arrived in Indiana, the Ku Klux Klan began an active campaign to win members north of the Mason-Dixon line. The Red Scare and race riots of 1919 led to the Klan's call for "100 percent Americanism" and a recruitment drive north of Dixie. Stephenson was a promoter and a salesman; the Klan needed both. He harbored dreams of becoming a powerful politician; the Klan offered him a base of support and a platform. By 1921 he was hustling, stumping, and recruiting for the organization.[2]

In 1922 Stephenson moved from Evansville to Indianapolis and began selling stock in a coal company and recruiting for the Klan. He found a town of friendly people, ready to buy his stock, believe his stories, and join his "patriotic" organization. Though Indianapolis did not seem threatened by Catholic and Jewish immigrants or African Americans, it was pocketed by ethnic neighborhoods—Irish on the southeast and near-west sides, Italians and Greeks on the east side, Jews on the south side, and blacks on the northwest side along Indiana Avenue. For many white Protestant residents of Indianapolis, these neighborhoods seemed to threaten the cozy rural ambiance of their town.[3]

The Klan did not import racism into Indianapolis; it simply articulated existing attitudes. It helped supply the language and rationale for racial, religious, and ethnic exclusion. In the early 1920s it joined with the Capitol Avenue Protective Association, various residential groups, and local politicians in an attempt to block African Americans from moving into white neighborhoods on the north side. And it supported all efforts to segregate Indianapolis schools.[4]

Blacks had long been segregated from whites in Indianapolis elementary schools, and many whites had assumed that there was no need for a separate black high school. White officials reasoned that with the absence of mandatory educational laws, few black parents would elect to send their children to high school. But they reasoned wrongly. By 1920 there were about eight hundred blacks in the city's high schools, and whites lobbied the school board to build a separate high school for black students. In late 1922 the school board responded, unanimously approving a proposal to build a high school for blacks. Placing the best possible spin on the plan, the board said the new school would mean more jobs for black teachers. But concern over blacks moving to the near-north side of the city and "invading white neighborhoods" lay behind the board's decision.

African Americans protested the board's action and appealed to the NAACP to champion their cause, but they were generally ignored by both groups. Their only success was a token, but highly symbolic, one. The school board had voted, again unanimously, to name the school Thomas Jefferson High School.

Blacks argued that an all-black school—if, in fact, there had to be one—should be named after a black hero, not a white slaveholder. The board relented, naming the school Crispus Attucks High School, after the African American who had been shot by British troops in the 1770 Boston Massacre.

Crispus Attucks was built in the heart of Frog Island, on West Street between Eleventh and Twelfth Streets, with the foul-smelling Central Canal close to its front doors and Fall Creek flowing lugubriously a few blocks away. The board appointed a black man, Matthias Nolcox, to serve as Attucks's first principal, and he hired a white man, Sergeant Frank Whitlow, to serve as the first instructor for the school's Reserve Officers' Training Corps. Both decisions sent a clear message: Attucks would be an African American school, staffed and run almost exclusively by African Americans, but for a sensitive military position a white face was essential.

Crispus Attucks opened its doors for its first students in September 1927, and from day one it was inadequate. The school was constructed to serve 1,000 students; more than 1,350 students enrolled at Crispus Attucks the first year, and the numbers increased in later years. But the school board expressed no concern. It had built a school for black high school students, which meant that all other high schools in the city were reserved for whites. Eighteen black students demanded the right to remain in their original schools, arguing that their degree plans entailed several subjects that were not offered at Attucks. The superintendent refused their requests and ordered them to attend Attucks.

The rise of the Klan and the construction of Crispus Attucks signaled an acceptance of segregation by white residents in Indiana's capital. Other cities followed Indianapolis's example. By the end of the decade Roosevelt High School was built in Gary and Lincoln High School in Evansville to satisfy segregationists. And housing in Indianapolis became even more restricted. African Americans attempting to move into white neighborhoods faced inflated housing prices, stingy bankers, and angry citizen groups.

A monument to racism, Crispus Attucks ironically was soon transformed into a symbol of black pride. It became an anchor for the community, a place where black children could be instructed by black teachers, learn about black history, and enjoy educational and social successes denied them in integrated schools. By 1930, when Russell A. Lane was named the new principal, the school had attracted a distinguished group of teachers, several with Ph.D. degrees, and served the community as a social center. During the next three decades it educated scores of talented African Americans, and if such jazz musicians as J. J. Johnson, Slide Hampton, Wes Montgomery, Jimmy Coe, and Jimmy Spaulding became nationally known, hundreds of other Attucks graduates became doctors, lawyers, educators, and community leaders.

In the decades after 1930, however, sports came to define the school. During the early part of the century, when blacks attended integrated Indianapolis high schools, a few participated in minor sports, but none played on the city's best basketball teams. The Senate Avenue YMCA, long a central institution in black Indianapolis, had nourished an interest in all sports, especially basketball, offering programs and schedules for youths and young men. The Senate Y guaranteed a deep pool of talent for Crispus Attucks. The problem for Attucks administrators was not talent; it was opponents. The white Indianapolis public schools refused to play Attucks, as did most other Indiana high schools. Instead of crosstown rivalries, Attucks had to compete against other all-black schools, often traveling hundreds of miles out of state for a game. In addition to Gary Roosevelt and Evansville Lincoln, it played schools in Kentucky, Ohio, Missouri, and as far away as Oklahoma.[5]

Eventually, a few Catholic schools and smaller rural schools agreed to play Attucks. Like Attucks, Indiana Catholic schools were members of the Klan's untouchables list, foreign places controlled by who knew what sort of nefarious forces. They had almost as much of a problem scheduling games as Attucks, and again, like Attucks, were not included under the umbrella of the Indiana High School Athletic Association, which sponsored state championships, ruled on infractions, and regulated competition. The rural schools were members of the IHSAA, but they discovered that a game against Attucks was an easy way to make money. "Those tiny rural schools loved to play Attucks," Indianapolis basketball authority Joe Wolfla recalled. "It was like the circus coming to town, like the Globetrotters coming to town." Men brought their families into town just to gawk at the dark-skinned strangers, then packed the gym to watch the game.

Confronted with such schools as Attucks, Gary Roosevelt, and Evansville Lincoln, the IHSAA adopted a curious Alice-in-Wonderland position. Led by the czar of Indiana high school sports, the dictatorial IHSAA head Arthur Trester, the organization did not bar individual black athletes from competition. Because only the largest cities had an all-black high school, African Americans living in smaller communities attended predominantly white high schools, and a few became basketball stars. In 1930 Dave DeJernette led Washington to the state championship, although in the official team photograph his image was badly cropped. And during the rest of the decade other blacks distinguished themselves on other championship teams.

But, insisted Trester, Attucks and the other all-black high schools presented an entirely different issue, one that transcended race. As he told a delegation of Indianapolis black community leaders in 1927, Crispus Attucks was not really a public school since it catered only to black students. And since it was not a public school it was not eligible to join the IHSAA. Trester's logic had the perfect symmetry of a catch-22: first, white officials forced Indianapolis blacks to attend a segregated school; then another white official defined them outside of the IHSAA because they attended a segregated school. It was curiouser and curiouser, but for fourteen years Trester refused to budge on the issue.[6]

Time and again, Indianapolis's most influential black leaders tried to get Trester to change his policy. Each time he refused. Throughout 1941 the pressure mounted on Trester to alter his position. Citizens petitioned for change, politicians introduced bills demanding change, ministers delivered sermons pleading for change, and editorials trumpeted the need to change. The issue had moved from an educational to political and moral realms. Finally, on December 20, 1941, in the patriotic days after Pearl Harbor, Trester gave in. The record of the Athletic Council meeting showed the passage of the following resolution: "Membership in the Association shall be open beginning August 15, 1942, to all public, private, parochial, colored and institutional high schools of the state offering and maintaining three or four years of high school work provided they meet the requirements of the Association and also subscribe to its rules and regulations."[7]

In language as dry as a spoonful of flour, Crispus Attucks—and other all-black and Catholic high schools—were welcomed into the IHSAA.

By the time Oscar Robertson tried out for the basketball team, the Crispus Attucks Tigers had become one of the premier teams in the state. And as much as any man, Ray Crowe, the head coach who would decide if Oscar had a future on the team, had been responsible for Attucks's rise to prominence. The players fighting for a spot on the team had nicknamed Crowe the "Razor" because it was his job to cut players, many of them very talented. Of course, they did not call him that to his face; when they addressed him it was simply "Mr. Crowe" or sometimes "Coach Crowe." He was a midsize, powerfully built man who commanded great respect and some fear. Although he treated his players like members of his own family, he assumed the role of the patriarch—approachable, fair, but not a pal. "Coach Crowe was a nice guy, soft-spoken, but he was stern," Bill Swatts recalled in the mid-1990s. "He didn't take any crap, and that was something that you knew beforehand. He had the ability to discipline kids. I still call him Mr. Crowe to this day."

In some ways Crowe was trapped between two generations of black men, burning with a desire both to fit in and be accepted by whites and to slash through all racial barriers to victory. In public he could never show how much he wanted to win; he had to play the role of the gracious loser. But the mild courtside exterior was a mask. He was never, ever content with second place. He was a competitor.

Ray Crowe had grown up surrounded by white faces—some covered with white hoods. He was born outside Franklin, Indiana, in 1915—the same year as the rebirth of the Ku Klux Klan. As a child he witnessed hooded Klansmen in downtown Franklin, but they never seemed threatening. Most were farmers, men whose sons were his playmates, whose farms were near his father's, whose wives cooked communal meals with his mother after harvests. Until Crowe was in high school, his family was the sole factor in the growth of the black population in Franklin. He was one of ten children, the eldest of eight boys. "I was half-way through school before another black family moved into town," he remembered. "We were the only two black families. All my friends were white."[8]

Crowe maintained that most of the prejudice he faced in his early years was incidental. He learned the places he was not allowed to go and the things he was not allowed to do, then avoided the first and did not try the second. But his high school coach taught him that there were no restrictions—no closed doors or stay-away signs—in the world of sports. Years later he vividly recalled one basketball game. He was in eighth grade, and his team was playing an all-white Franklin team. "A big kid was guarding me, really working me over. I was strong and athletic, and I didn't worry about anyone beating up on me, but I just didn't want to do anything to embarrass my coach or the team." During halftime, Crowe's coach told him not to back down; if his opponent wanted to play rough, he should play rough. "Early in the second half I drove my man up into the bleachers and got him off my back. It worked. The player stopped the dirty stuff. That was a valuable lesson learned, one I later taught to my players."

For Ray Crowe, education and sports provided an avenue to escape the drudgery of farm chores. At the appropriately named Whiteland, he was a standout athlete, and after graduation he attended Indiana Central University. Again surrounded by white students, he excelled in the classroom and on the basketball court. After graduating in the top tenth of his class, he obtained a job as a sweeper with International Harvester, but he was soon promoted to a position as a crane operator.

During World War II, Emory James, a fraternity brother who was the principal of Indianapolis's all-black School 17, offered Crowe a job teaching math and physical education. Trained as a teacher and longing to coach, he accepted the position, which placed him for the first time in his life in an all-black environment. It was not a world where he was initially comfortable. When he was young his father used to take him and his brothers on Saturday outings to Indiana Avenue, where he felt out of place surrounded by other African Americans. The farms around Franklin, the neat campus of Indiana Central, the plant of International Harvester—these open, controlled, overwhelmingly white environments he knew. But a black ghetto was something very different—a crowded, seemingly uncontrolled place.

"Those first few weeks were tough and I could not imagine things becoming easier," he later said. All his students were in eighth grade, but some were sixteen or seventeen years old, more men than youths, with strong bodies and quick tempers. Crowe was as exotic to them as they were to him, and they challenged him. He preached the virtues of education; in their actions more than their words, they questioned his naive faith. Where would education take them? After all, the only ticket it had given Crowe admitted him into their west-side ghetto. His college degree was valueless at the white schools in Indianapolis. Unable to break through their reserve, Crowe considered resigning. "I knew I could do other things, and I didn't need the frustration," he recalled.

But he stayed, finding a way to discipline his students and preach his gospel of education. Sports became central to his mission. They had gotten him off the farm and aided in the development of his seven other brothers, so it was logical to think that they could provide a sense of self-worth to the pupils he instructed. By the mid-1940s he had developed an intramural basketball program for junior high students, which allowed him to locate and develop the best young talent. Then in 1948 Crispus

Attucks principal Russell Lane offered him a job as a high school teacher and assistant basketball coach.

Two frustrating years followed. The problem was the coaching philosophy of head coach Fitzhugh Lyons. Like Principal Lane and Athletic Director Alonzo Watford, Lyons had been well schooled in a benign brand of race relations. For them the end result of interracial athletic competition was social harmony. Black athletes were black ambassadors who promoted goodwill and understanding. When Attucks played against a small rural high school, Lane would travel with the team and work the crowd. The short, conservatively dressed, bespectacled man moved through the bleachers, shaking a hand here, engaging in a brief conversation there. He concentrated on making friends, not watching the game. On the court were athletes he had personally instructed to play like gentlemen—no arguing with officials, no belittling opponents, no behind-the-back passes or Globetrotter antics. He measured victory not by the score at the end of the game, but by the impression his team made on the locals. Perhaps, he reasoned, exposure to well-behaved black players would cut through the thick atmosphere of racism and misunderstanding.[9]

Lyons and Watford shared Lane's beliefs, and they probably thought Crowe did as well. Several people close to Attucks at the time believed that Crowe's light skin and background in rural Indiana accounted for his employment. Here, Lane might have thought, was a black man in touch with the realities of towns like Amo and Sheridan, comfortable in the crackerbox gyms of the countryside.

Lane was correct in assuming that Crowe knew his way around the back roads of Indiana; but he was wrong if he believed that the coach shared his approach to sports. Although sportsmanship was vitally important to him, Crowe also felt winning was important. Athletes felt better about themselves—and opponents respected them more—when they played hard and won.

For two years Crowe watched Lyons and Lane labor to make gentlemen out of basketball players. Lyons was a tough ex–Big Ten football player who wanted to win, but years of coaching in a system that demanded certain racial accommodations had begun to wear him down, and his coaching philosophy had become more conservative. "Keep both feet on the ground when you shoot and pass," Lyons instructed. "Don't get too close to your man on defense. Make the safe pass. Take the good shot." It was a game of don'ts—don't showboat, don't argue, don't show aggression, don't be too good. Attucks played with a yoke. What was remarkable was that the teams often won. But they could never move into the elite class. After losing early in sectional play in 1950, Crowe expressed his frustration. "Don't worry," Lyons told him. "It's better to lose now than later."

The next season all that began to change. Lyons retired from coaching, and Crowe became head coach. If "don't" did not disappear from the Attucks philosophy, it was balanced by a greater sense of freedom. "I didn't want [the players] to be afraid to try something out of fear they'd be pulled from the game," Crowe said. He also wanted the best players on his team. Lyons's teams had been characterized by players from more middle-class black families, often referred to as "north siders" because they lived blocks away from the stench of the canal and Frog Island. Crowe, however, evinced an interest in the poorer and "hungrier" athletes, many of whom had only recently arrived in Indianapolis with their families from the rural South.[10]

That year Attucks began to win—big. The 1950–51 team upset perennial basketball power Anderson and made it to the state finals before losing to Evansville Reitz. That game galled Crowe. Not only had he allowed Lane to give one of his "gentlemen speeches" to his players before the game, but he himself had let his players down. He had not taught them how to play an aggressive man-to-man defense, and he had not worked them hard enough. He felt they lacked conditioning. "I told myself after the game that we would be back, and that next time there would be no excuses. Next time we would be ready for any sort of game. Next time we would win."

He hoped next time would be the following year. His 1951–52 team was loaded with Frog Island talent, including Dust Bowl players Willie "Dill" Gardner, Hallie Bryant, and Bailey "Flap" Robertson. Many of the players were a level or two poorer than those who had played for Lyons. In fact, Crowe had to struggle to keep Gardner, his finest player, on the team. Gardner's mother was chronically short of money, and when basketball season ended, Dill demonstrated a marked tendency to quit coming to school and get a job to pay family bills. Crowe talked to him, visited his home, explained to him and his mother that education was the only sure road out of poverty. To bolster Dill's sagging spirits, Crowe gave him small gifts. After one spring flight Crowe presented Dill with some underwear and several pairs of argyle socks. Years later Dill Gardner still remembered the acts of kindness: "Argyle socks were popular back then and I remember walking around in those socks. I was so proud."[11]

The poorer players were also the hungrier ones. Gone were Lyons's perfect gentlemen, replaced by relentlessly aggressive athletes who dunked in practice, pushed the ball down the court, and got into their opponents' faces. "They were raw at times, but tough," Assistant Coach Al Spurlock said. "Attucks fans loved their brand of basketball." They seemed to capture the energy of the Avenue, a spirit that mixed resentment with restrictions and pride in themselves. When they went to away games they packed their own meals rather than face rejection at a roadside diner, but they cut a measure of revenge on the court, beating teams by twenty, thirty, forty, fifty points.

Flap Robertson best represented the post-Lyons Attucks player. Born in Tennessee and a product of the World War II black migration from the South, he displayed conduct on the court that fell considerably short of the Lyons ideal. His game was an expression of his own inner feelings. Talking about his fellow Dust Bowl players, he said, "We took our basketball seriously. I know I always tried to invent some new way of showing up the guy who was guarding me. We hated to lose, hated to have someone make us look bad." In Attucks games he played the same way, which brought him into conflict with his coach. "Flap had a personality that was irritating, not only to me but to other players," Crowe claimed. "He taunted players. Once we were playing in a Christmas tournament at Lafayette Jefferson. Flap was taunting a player, and I yanked him out of the game. The next week I suspended him, and he didn't come to practice, and he knew that he wouldn't play. I had him in my homeroom, and he was ticked off. Wouldn't even talk to me until I let him back on the team."[12]

Flap's temper and finding a place to eat on the road were minor problems, however, compared to biased officials. In most games Attucks's superiority rendered the officials superfluous. But in close contests the officials could swing a game to Attucks's opponents. Against powerful South Bend Central, for example, Attucks had a five-point lead with less than two minutes remaining in the game. On their last five possessions Attucks's players were whistled for fouls, giving South Bend a three-point victory. "I'd never seen anything so blatantly unfair in all my life," commented reporter Bob Collins. "Five fouls in a couple of minutes on every possession? How could that happen? . . . That game was refereed purely on the basis of race." "I guess I knew something was up when I heard the referee call a foul on number thirteen," recalled Gardner, whose number was thirteen. "I was sitting, fouled-out, on the bench. So, I stood up and raised my hand. 'I'm right here,' I said."[13]

The 1951–52 season ended in another disappointment. Attucks lost early in sectional play. On the west side it felt as if Santa Claus had died. Hallie Bryant knew what the loss meant: "People in our community had very little to look forward to, but one of the things they dearly loved was Crispus Attucks basketball. During that part of the year folks built their evenings around where and how they were going to watch and listen to our ball games. We were their pride and joy and we knew it. The worst thing we could do was lose."[14]

The next season, 1952–53, the Tigers won their sectional and regional tournaments and advanced into the state semifinal round. There they played Shelbyville, a town south of Indianapolis. With the score tied in the fourth quarter, Shelbyville's coach ordered his team to stall for the last shot. At the 1:59 mark Attucks reserve John Bridgeforth tipped the ball from the hands of Norman Poe and broke with it toward the basket. Held at the start of his dash, Bridgeforth was brushed again as he went up for a shot. To most reporters it looked like a foul, but the referee signaled jump ball. Attucks controlled the tip and worked for a good shot. With less than a minute to play, Hallie Bryant cut for the basket with a clear shot. As he left the ground, he was sandwiched by two Shelbyville players and knocked to the floor. His shot bounded off the rim and was tipped in by Winford O'Neal.[15]

Once again a whistle stopped the action as referee Stan Dubis waved off O'Neal's basket. Incredibly, he called charging on Bryant and gave Shelbyville's Jim Playmate two free throws. Attucks clawed back, forcing what appeared to be a turnover, but once again the referees awarded the ball—and the game—to Shelbyville.

"Sportsmen Shocked at 'Fantastic' Call," was the banner headline of the *Indianapolis Recorder*. The "wrong, raw and inexcusable" call bothered reporters across the state, but black journalists were the most incensed. "Many Negro young people, and others who are trying to believe in a democratic America," noted editorialist Charles S. Preston, "are asking this week: 'Is it always going to be true that officials will take the close games away from Attucks, the close fights away from Negro boxers? Has a person with a dark skin got a chance for fair play?'" They were questions that stalked the halls of Crispus Attucks and formed the basis for hundreds of conversations along Indiana Avenue.[16]

Of all the players, Hallie Bryant took the game the most personally. "I can't think about anything else," he said a few days later. "It was the awfulest thing that ever happened to me." He discussed the controversial call as if it were a train wreck. "I didn't foul anybody. I guess this will be with me the rest of my life."[17]

But perhaps Ray Crowe had the most difficult time coming to terms with the loss. The Shelbyville game stayed on his mind during the off-season. The most he would say to the press was "Hallie was hacked," but privately the game ate at him. He was responsible for the Evansville Reitz loss, he reasoned, but the Shelbyville game was simple larceny. The call made him even more grimly determined to win a championship. "Shelbyville ended any illusions I had that it would be easy," he recalled. "I knew that the team with the best players might not win. But I had faith. All we needed were players good enough to take the officials out of the game."

Chapter Three

MAKING THE TEAM

Ray Crowe had not encouraged Oscar Robertson to try out for the varsity basketball team in the fall of 1953, but he was well aware of the young player's reputation. He had watched Oscar lead his eighth-grade School 17 team to the city championship. The final game had been played at Arsenal Technical High School and drew a good crowd. Most of the players were a little rattled and tried to demonstrate more talent than they had. But not Oscar. He played within himself, giving the impression that he had more than he showed. What impressed Crowe was not that he had "a lot of basketball ability," but that he had "a lot of leadership ability." It was as if Oscar knew things about the game that the others would never know enough to even think about.

Some people called him "Little Flap," but Oscar was no clone of his older brother. Bailey Robertson Jr. was almost professionally gregarious, quick to smile, laugh, and talk. If he was occasionally volatile on the court and demonstrated a tendency to irritate opposing players . . . well, his friends said, "that was just Flap. He didn't mean anything by it." Oscar, however, was as introverted as Bailey was extroverted. "He was just so shy," Crowe recalled. "Even after he became our star player he was shy. It was like pulling teeth to get him into a team picture. And as soon as a game was over, he showered and left fast so he would not have to talk to reporters."

But in one way Oscar and Bailey were similar: their desire to win. They were intense competitors with different styles. What Bailey would do with words, Oscar would do with a look or a slight gesture. And during the tryouts Oscar competed as hard as he ever had before. "I played my best basketball when I went out for the team," he said. "I was playing with the second stringers, against players who should have beaten Shelbyville the year before. They had played against the best in the state, and I felt I had to be good to be noticed." He was. When the Razor made his final cuts, Oscar was still on the squad.

During the tryouts and even into the early season, the Attucks team lacked a defining character. The players who had forged Attucks's reputation were gone—Hallie Bryant to Indiana University, Flap Robertson to Indiana Central, Willie Gardner to the Harlem Globetrotters. The best of the returning players had mostly been role players the year before. Overall, the team seemed to lack height and a consistent scorer. Even the perennially optimistic and supportive *Indianapolis Recorder* reporters expressed doubts about the team. "If there's a Hallie Bryant on the squad, he is as yet undiscovered," commented one reporter. And when he asked an Attucks student for the scuttlebutt about the team, the answer was, "Oh, they say it won't get anywhere."[1]

The only thing about the team that was certain was that once again it would play no real home games. The school with no "gymnasium, football field [or] track worthy of the name" would play every game either in its opponents' gyms or at neutral sites. This awkward situation made scheduling a nightmare. Attucks had to arrange its "home" games to conform to the schedules of Butler University or the various local high schools. As a result it might play three games in four days, then not have another game for a week or ten days. Indiana boasted the largest high school gyms in the nation, but one of its finest teams was without a home court.[2]

In Attucks's first game of the season, the situation became a painful reality for Oscar Robertson. The team was scheduled to play Fort Wayne North in Arsenal Technical High School's gym. Coach Crowe told his players the time they needed to arrive at Tech, but not how to get there. Too shy to inquire, Oscar decided to take a crosstown bus. What might seem like a minor inconvenience was complicated by the city's turf divisions. It was potentially a risky proposition for a black teenage male from the west side to board a bus for another part of the city. Forty-five years later Oscar still vividly recalled that bus ride. "I didn't know how to get there. I had to ask a bus driver how to get to my first varsity game. I remember because some guy pulled a knife on me on the bus. I didn't know what to do, and I sure didn't want to get cut before my first game. I just walked away."

The game began with Oscar sitting on the bench beside the other reserves. Three minutes into the contest Coach Crowe sent in "Little Flap." Oscar was about the same height as his older brother and wore the same number forty-three on his jersey, but once in the game he did not remind people of Flap. Some said he played like Hallie Bryant, others like Willie Gardner, and all agreed he was "headed for top stardom." He scored fifteen points from his forward position and played with a poise unexpected of a sophomore.[3]

The performance made Oscar a starter and gave Attucks supporters more confidence in their inexperienced team. Playing on the road, the Tigers easily defeated Fort Wayne Central and Sheridan. Even more than before, out-of-town schools regarded an Attucks matchup as a money game and a focal point of the season. Arriving in small towns in buses and automobiles, Attucks players and students became objects of intense curiosity. "It was like we were from outer space," recalled a former student. "I mean, I would hear their comments to each other: 'Look at that one, he's really black. And that one, she's as light as my mother's coffee.' Some just gawked open-mouthed. But, hell, I was sort of surprised that they weren't chewing on a piece of straw." Another student, a former cheerleader, also remembered the "long stares. . . . Everywhere we went folks would wait for our buses to arrive and then follow us into the gym. I remember one night this little boy came down and wanted to talk to the cheerleaders. He was a friendly little lad and we had a good chat. He stayed right with us through the start of the game, and a few minutes into the contest I felt this scratching at my arm. I turned and looked, but I didn't see anything. A little later there it was again. That little boy was scratching my arm with his fingernail and then putting it into his mouth. 'It isn't chocolate,' I told him. 'It's my skin, the same as yours, I'm just darker than you are.'"[4]

With another outstanding team and games aplenty on its schedule, the main concern in the African American community in Indianapolis returned to the subject of officials. "Will We Be 'Robbed' Again?" was the headline of an *Indianapolis Recorder* editorial. Would officials once again prevent Attucks from reaching its goal? The belief was strong that it had happened three straight years. "The thing has affected them so powerfully that they halfway wish Attucks was not good enough to be a strong contender." But the team was that good, so the fears persisted. And with good reason. As in previous years, the Indiana Officials Association had excluded all blacks from membership—and "as long as the referees keep jimcrow in their organization, an ugly doubt will remain." Ray Crowe, however, refused to give voice to his own concerns. "Get a big lead and keep it," he told his players, "and the referees will play no role in the game."[5]

But officials were not the only people bent on influencing a game's outcome. Attucks basketball generated passionate interest; the game was central to the players' lives, central to the social life of the west-side community, and of keen interest to local gamblers. On December 8, 1953, eight days before Attucks's game with Arsenal Tech, David Huff, a Tech guard who was walking home after basketball practice, noticed a parked mud-splattered automobile. As he moved past the car, three black men in their mid-to-late twenties leaped out and surrounded him. One grabbed his collar; the other two poked him with knives. "You're Dave Huff, Tech's long shooter ain't you," one said. Huff nodded his head yes. "You're a good shot, but you better not play too good [against Attucks]. If you make one single point . . . we'll come back and cut you wide open."[6]

The assault and threats received front-page attention in Indianapolis newspapers. Some Tech officials—usually not mentioned by name—questioned the wisdom of playing Attucks, suggesting that if the game could cause death threats perhaps the two teams should not play each other. Although racial stereotypes of knife-wielding blacks were not mentioned specifically, they seemed to hover between the lines of the stories. Tech had not played Attucks for two years, and that game had been in the state tournament. Now the Huff episode increased the already palpable tension between the east-side and west-side schools.[7]

Other threats followed. Huff's mother and coach both received telephone calls with the same message: if Dave Huff played he would regret it. It was an odd drama. Why Huff, reporters wondered. He was not Tech's best—or even second-best—player. He was simply a steady role player, unlikely to decide the outcome of a game. Police were also baffled. Gamblers did not appear to be behind the threats. But relations between the two schools became even more icy than usual, and police detailed strategies to keep the races separated at the game.[8]

Not even the police, however, could stop the campaign of threats. Threatening notes, penciled on toilet paper, arrived at the homes of Huff and Tech coach Charles P. Maas: "Keep Huff and [Don] Sexson out of the ball game. We mean it." A few days before the game, Ray Crowe also received an unsigned note written on a piece of scratch paper: "Do not play Winifred [*sic*] O'Neal or William Mason if you value their lives. I have all my possessions bet on the game, including my car and house and I want to see Tech win."[9]

Nor was Oscar left out of the battle of threats. He received a call that worried his father but did not much concern him. "I didn't think much about it," he said. "It was probably just some gambler who just wanted to give me something to think about." But the episode ended the innocence of Oscar's first varsity year and seemed to interrupt the flow of the season. Attucks continued its strong play, defeating South Bend Riley and hometown rival Broad Ripple before losing to Terre Haute Gerstmeyer, the state's top-ranked team. But these games were all contested in the shadow of the threats.

By mid-December the Attucks-Tech game—and the threats and counterthreats—was the leading story in Indianapolis. It had become "one of the most publicized games in Indiana high school basketball history," and by tip-off almost ten thousand spectators crowded into the bleachers of Butler Fieldhouse, establishing an attendance record for a regular-   season game in Indianapolis. Police stood patrol outside both teams' dressing rooms and followed the players to and from the court. Police, uniformed and plainclothed, stationed themselves throughout the fieldhouse. FBI agents, brought into the case when death threats were sent through the mail, also roamed about, asking questions and jotting notes. During warm-ups players nervously missed shots and glanced furtively at the stands. Of the five players whose lives had been threatened, only David Huff was not on the court. His parents and coach insisted that he take no chances and remain at home. He "cried like a baby" when told he could not play, Coach Maas told reporters.[10]

Given the tense atmosphere, a great basketball game would have seemed out of the question. And it was. Both teams shot well below 30 percent, threw away an exceptional number of passes, and looked equally ragged on offense and defense. Winford O'Neal, Attucks's leading scorer, made only two of fifteen field-goal attempts; the usually steady Harold Crenshaw, only one of ten. Tech's leading players also shot well below their season averages. The game was not so much about which team would play better, but which would play worse.[11]

One player, however, seemed oddly unaffected by the excitement of the night. Oscar Robertson, the youngest player on the court, scored the first basket of the game and played steadily throughout. He helped Attucks build a fourteen-point lead during the first two and a half quarters and made several crucial baskets when Tech rallied in the late-third and fourth quarters. More than anyone else, he was responsible for Attucks's 43-38 victory.

After the Tech game reporters rarely again referred to Oscar as "Little Flap." Nor did they often quote him. Unlike his older brother, he shot less frequently and far closer to the basket, but he made more. And he was just as guarded with his comments. If possible, he said nothing. If pressed, he said little. But quietly he was becoming the leader of the team. "There was just something about him, even then, that gave you more confidence," teammate Bill Scott recalled. "He had such great control, and I'm not talking about how he handled the basketball. He controlled himself. Controlled the game."

Yet in one way Robertson was like his teammates. They all lacked consistency. In an effort to place a positive spin on the situation, journalists applauded Attucks as the team without a star player. Each game, they noted, it seemed as if a different player led his team. Some nights it was O'Neal, Sheddrick Mitchell, or Crenshaw working inside; other nights it was Mason raining in shots from outside. Increasingly it was Oscar scoring on drives, pull-up jumpers, and free throws. But even his game ran hot and cold—one game fifteen or eighteen points, the next three or four. Given the team's inconsistent play—and hovering threat of bad calls—losses seemed inevitable.

Trying to give his team more stability, midway through the season Ray Crowe moved Oscar from forward to guard. He wanted the ball in Oscar's hands. The first-ever Indianapolis invitational holiday tournament demonstrated the wisdom of Crowe's decision. Attucks was matched against Shortridge in the first round of the tournament, and most of Oscar's teammates played as if they were still stuffed from Christmas and New Year celebrations. And, in fact, they had overeaten in their New Year's pregame meal. Left unsupervised and with an open account by Coach Crowe, they had helped themselves to seconds and thirds. That night at Butler Fieldhouse, most played with a sluggish disinterest. O'Neal connected on only one of nine shots, Mason on four of nineteen. Oscar, who had demonstrated more restraint at lunch, quietly took over the game. He took ten shots, made eight, and finished the game with nineteen points. More important, his steady play kept Shortridge from mounting a comeback.[12]

The next afternoon, however, Oscar made only one field-goal attempt, though Attucks easily defeated Manual. The victory set up an Attucks-Tech rematch, one with Dave Huff but without death threats and FBI agents. Unlike the first game, when Tech kids played the first half as if they were searching the stands for snipers, Tech started fast. "I told them they lost the last time because they were afraid when the game started," Tech coach Charlie Maas said. "I didn't have to fire them up for this one. They were ready." For most of the first three quarters Tech outshot, outscrambled, and outplayed Attucks, leading by six at the quarter, nine at the half, and fifteen with just over three minutes to play in the third quarter.[13]

Then Robertson and O'Neal took over the game. With less than three minutes remaining Tech led by five points. But a driving layup by Oscar and a hook by O'Neal cut the lead to one point. Once again, however, several crucial calls by the referees went against Attucks, and Tech survived the rally. In the locker room the usually uncomplaining Crowe quietly voiced his concerns about the officiating. Throughout the game, he lamented, the officials seemed inclined to call touch fouls on his team and ignore his opponent's more blatant infractions. Reporter Bob Collins of the *Indianapolis Star* sympathized: "While these sports pages have never attempted to side either for or against officials at any time, no matter the situation, it must be reported that there were those who agreed."[14]

Soon the bad calls drifted into the background as Attucks faced even more serious problems. Early in 1954 a rash of illnesses and injuries attacked Attucks's players like a plague. Sheddrick Mitchell, a powerful forward, had injured his knee in a football game, and an operation kept him out of the first third of the season. Just as he began to find his game, Willie Merriweather—Mitchell's replacement—injured his knee. He too had damaged it playing football and aggravated it playing basketball. Late in January a surgeon at General Hospital repaired cartilage damage and speculated that Merriweather would be able to return to the team in time for the state tournament, but Crowe had his doubts. The prospect of two of Attucks's tallest inside men playing at less than full strength did not bode well for the team, but worse was yet to come. In a game against Indianapolis Sacred Heart, Winford O'Neal, one of the finest centers in the state, injured his right knee. For more than a week he did not see a physician, hoping that it was just a bad sprain. In the next two games he played in obvious pain, and in a loss against Indianapolis Howe he twisted the knee again in a midcourt scramble and had to be helped to the locker room. Finally he got it examined. He had torn the lateral cartilage, a diagnosis that abruptly ended his Attucks career.[15]

Although Attucks was still ranked in the top ten teams of the state, reporters commented that the injuries to O'Neal and Merriweather would effectively end the team's season. In addition to losing its most valuable senior, it had lost its entire inside game. Ray Crowe realized that the loss of O'Neal, his best post player, dramatically changed the balance of his team, and he made radical offensive and defensive adjustments. On offense, he scrapped the post setup and replaced it with a three-guard perimeter arrangement. Robertson, Bill Mason, and Norman Crowe (no relation to Ray Crowe) handled the ball while Sheddrick Mitchell and Harold Crenshaw took their positions in the corners. This setup de-emphasized height and power in favor of passing, ballhandling, and quickness. With the middle free, players could drive for scores or make quick cuts to the basket. The offense particularly suited the skills of Robertson and Mitchell; Oscar's driving ability often forced double teams, and Sheddrick was adept at cutting for the ball. On defense Attucks turned up the pressure with full-court presses and close man-to-man defense.[16]

It took time to adjust to the losses of Merriweather and O'Neal and to learn the new system. Crowe lengthened practices, driving his players to exhaustion. Sometimes they were flat for games. During late January and early February, the Tigers struggled. Indianapolis Howe and Hammond Noll defeated them, and they only narrowly beat Indianapolis Shortridge, Mishawaka, and Indianapolis Washington. But as the state tournament approached, the team began to play with more confidence, and the rumor of its demise seemed premature. *Indianapolis Recorder* columnist Charles Preston suspected that race had much to do with sportswriters' views: "There was an eagerness in certain parts of town to see Attucks fall. Maybe this infected the writers, and disturbed their sense of balance." But in defense of the sportswriters, it seemed unlikely that any team could lose two starters—one its leading scorer and rebounder—and still be a serious threat to win any kind of tournament.[17]

Yet by the end of the regular season Attucks appeared as strong as ever. The emergence of Robertson and Mitchell as scorers had even white sportswriters reversing their stand. After watching Attucks's pressing defense befuddle Indianapolis Cathedral, *Indianapolis Star* writer Bert West observed, "Note to those who are saying injury-riddled Crispus Attucks has reached the end of the trail: Please omit flowers. The Tigers ain't dead yet." In fact, when Attucks entered the state tournament with a 17-4 record, sportswriters believed it was still one of the two best schools in the city and looked forward to another Attucks-Tech game in the sectional finals. And for the first time in the decade, Attucks was placed into the weakest bracket. Its leading rivals—Tech, Howe, Cathedral, and Shortridge—were all in the other bracket.[18]

"The state tourney marked the official end of winter along the Avenue," one black west-side resident recalled. "It might be cold as hell, the wind might be real sharp, but the tourney—the thought that Attucks might go all the way—made walking along the Avenue feel like a spring stroll." The advertisements in the *Indianapolis Recorder* registered the mood. "ONE—TWO—THREE—FOUR, WHO ARE WE FOR . . . ATTUCKS"— 22nd St. Cigar Store. "Attucks! Attucks! All the Way"—Dave's Market. "Roll! You Tigers, Roll!"—Jack's Upholstery. "Come On, Attucks! Load 'Em Up, Haul 'Em Away, We're Pulling For You All The Way"—Spurling Trucking Co. The same message, expressed in various forms, filled pages of the *Recorder*. Liquor stores and furniture stores, mattress companies and moving companies, pharmacies, bars, beauty shops, and bakeries—in a civic mantra they vented their incantations. Crispus Attucks was their team, their hope, their promise of better things to come.[19]

The advertisements filled the back pages of the *Recorder*. In the front pages another story spoke to the importance of basketball to Indianapolis's black and white communities. After the Tech incident, Indianapolis police mounted a thorough crackdown on Indiana Avenue gambling sites, reversing their traditional laissez-faire policy. Week after week the *Recorder* printed accounts of the police raids. After an investigation, the paper reported that "cigar stores, smoke shops, hangouts, and night clubs popularly regarded as dives, have been closed tight, their bolted doors and dark interiors announcing eloquently in sign language 'Closed for Business,' at least temporarily." Some westside residents blamed the raids on politics, but others insisted that the Tech affair made white Indianapolis more sensitive to the issue. In either case, the raids only drove gamblers further underground. They did not stop the activity.[20]

Sixteen teams trudged to Butler Fieldhouse for the Indianapolis sectional. The first round was played on Wednesday, the second round on Friday, the semifinals and finals on Saturday. Most of the winning teams stayed at Butler University during the tournament. Not Attucks players. They played and, win or lose, went home for the night. Attucks was also treated differently in another way. Beneath the fieldhouse bleachers was a room with several baskets. The other teams got a chance to use the room to warm up before their games, but Attucks never saw it. Oscar Robertson played his entire career without even being aware the room existed.

But Attucks hardly needed to warm up for its first few games. It coasted past Ben Davis and Lawrence Central to make it to the Saturday games. Another easy victory against Broad Ripple set up a third meeting with Tech, this time for the sectional championship. Before the game Ray Crowe stressed the importance of taking the referees out of the game, and that was exactly what his players did. Before the contest was five minutes old, Attucks led 12-0, and Tech did not make a basket from the field during the first quarter. With a comfortable lead, the Tigers settled into a deliberate offense to reduce turnovers and use the clock. The Tech players had no response. "Attucks left little doubt about its supremacy," noted the *Indianapolis Star*'s basketball writer Bert West.[21]

After the game Attucks players showered and went home. There were no wild celebrations, not even much talking. His players "made up their minds a long time ago that they'd beat Tech if they ever got the chance again," Crowe told reporters. Not only did they know they could defeat Tech, they wanted to prove it. Throughout the early rounds they had rooted for their rival, hoping that no upset would prevent the rematch. Clearly the losses of O'Neal and Merriweather had not dimmed their confidence. In fact, Crowe suggested, rather the opposite. The other players felt they had something to prove, and winning their third sectional crown in four years was only the first step.[22]

But if Crowe and his players did not dwell on the importance of the Tech game, Attucks's supporters did. It had been, as many realized, more than a game. Watching the game from the bleachers, *Indianapolis Recorder* editorialist and Attucks Spanish teacher Andrew W. Ramsey described the climate of "poorly concealed racism." Despite the fact that Tech started two blacks on its team, it was viewed as "the great white hope," and Ramsey observed one six- or seven-year-old white boy call another white youth a "nigger lover" for applauding a good Attucks play. For those watching the game, Ramsey realized, the struggle on the court only mirrored a larger struggle off the court. That was why "Negroes, who daily take a beating from the white man in industry, in business, in religion and in their living conditions were jubilant to see a symbol of white supremacy bite the dust."[23]

Other black leaders in Indianapolis were more hopeful. Although he was familiar with America's and Indianapolis's long history of racism, Fred A. Parker saw signs of progress. He saw officials treating Attucks more fairly, blacks playing on the other city teams, white fans cheering the successes of black athletes. And he saw men and women, white and black, "fighting for the cause of justice and humanity." Parker's optimism reflected the general tone of the *Indianapolis Recorder*. Repeatedly in editorials journalists emphasized the theme of progress, trying to convince their readers that the city's white residents really did consider Crispus Attucks "Indianapolis's team." Even Ramsey agreed that the situation had improved over the past decade, but he cautioned against naive optimism. Don't be influenced by a few basketball games, he warned. "We have not yet reached the position which may be called heaven."[24]

While editorialists debated the meaning of Attucks's victories, Crowe took his team to the regional. As usual, the rural schools in Attucks's regional presented a motivation problem. After defeating their city rivals, players struggled to get up for teams they knew they should beat. A reporter described Attucks's morning game against Fortville as "one of the poorest games of the season both on offense and defense." But led by Robertson, the Tigers still won by ten points. The evening final against Alexandria was an equally tame affair. Although the game was close for a quarter and a half, an eight-point spurt put Attucks out of reach.[25]

The semifinal round generated more excitement, particularly for the contrasts it presented. Sportswriters expected Attucks and Milan to meet—Attucks the large, urban, all-black school; Milan the tiny, rural, all-white school. Reporters constantly referred to Milan as the Cinderella team, and so to some extent it was. Increasingly, Indiana basketball had been dominated by larger schools from Evansville, Anderson, Lafayette, Muncie, and South Bend. Milan was different. Pronounced "MY-lun," the town was nestled in the rolling farmland northwest of Cincinnati. The roughly eleven hundred people who lived there spent most of their time thinking about the practical concerns of their hog, tobacco, poultry, and cattle enterprises, or their jobs in the region's factories, but during the winter thoughts turned to basketball. Although only 161 students—73 boys—were enrolled in Milan High School, in the 1953 state tournament their team advanced all the way to the state finals before losing to the eventual champion, South Bend Central. Eight players, including four starters, returned for the following year.[26]

"Milan's story is almost as old as the state tourney," commented basketball reporter Bob Collins. Small town, tiny school, five white farm boys who were unfamiliar with stoplights, let alone neon lights, striving to outlast the other 750 schools that had entered the state tournament. But, once again, the Indianapolis story captured as much attention during the week before the semifinals. The question was: if all was gravy with the Milans of the state, what was wrong with the teams in the largest city in Indiana? The Indianapolis semifinals were played at Butler, a court familiar to Indianapolis teams; indeed, it was practically Attucks's home court. But no school from the capital had ever won a state tourney. Every year this badge of shame seemed more noticeable.[27]

Milan played the Montezuma Aztecs in the first semifinal game. Montezuma, a school of only seventy-nine pupils—thirty-six boys—and no gym, was cast in the role of the giant killer. But in the battle between a puny Goliath and a dwarf David, there was no upset. Milan capitalized on an opening spurt and a closing freeze to beat the Aztecs by ten points. When the game ended, Milan's coach Marvin Wood allowed his players to watch part of the next game before busing them off to a postgame meal and back to the Pennsylvania Hotel for some rest.[28]

While the Milan kids ate and rested, the Attucks players were clawing to stay in the tourney. The Attucks-Columbus contest was a ferocious, high-scoring affair. For two quarters the teams exchanged leads in an exceptionally fast, tight game. At the half Attucks led by a single point. In the third quarter Columbus caught fire while Attucks struggled. Harold Crenshaw fouled out, his teammates missed shots, and Columbus opened a fourteen-point lead on the strength of a twenty-three-point quarter. In the last quarter Robertson's drives and Bill Mason's jump shots rallied Attucks. Repeatedly, Oscar's slashes to the basket drew fouls. Columbus's center fouled out, and toward the end of the game the team's leading scorer followed him to the bench. With four and a half minutes left in the game, Columbus held a three-point lead and went into a stall. It failed. Attucks tied the game, fell behind by a point, then went ahead by two. For the rest of the game Robertson controlled the ball on offense. Columbus tied the score; Oscar drove, was fouled, and made both free throws.

Columbus once again leveled the game; Oscar once again drove, forced a foul, and put Attucks up by one. With only seconds remaining, Columbus missed a final shot.[29]

It had been the highest-scoring game in the history of the Indianapolis semifinals, and Attucks players straggled, exhausted, toward their locker room. But they had only hours to eat and rest before playing Milan in the evening game.

Like many games Attucks played against small, rural schools, race dominated the thinking of many of the spectators. No whites attended Attucks; no blacks lived in Milan. No players on either team mentioned the contrast, but they heard the comments as they ate their meals and took their warm-up shots. "When we went out to dinner that night," recalled Milan star Bobby Plump, "an unusual number of people followed us around. One of the frequent remarks we heard was, 'C'mon Milan, beat those niggers.'" And an Attucks player remembered hearing a fan at the game yell, "If you can't stand the heat, get back in the kitchen."[30]

Maybe Attucks's players had not fully recovered from their afternoon game; perhaps Milan was a better team. Certainly the little school that could, did. Milan started fast, shot 60 percent in the first half, captured a comfortable lead, and successfully controlled the pace of the game in the second half. Plump was superb, leading both teams with twenty-eight points. Robertson led Attucks with twenty-two points. "[Oscar] was pretty fluid and a heck of a basketball player when he was a sophomore," Plump later said. "I'm glad we got him when he was a sophomore and not a senior."[31]

Milan went on to the state finals, defeating powerful Muncie Central when Plump hit a last-second jumper. It was the most famous shot in the history of Indiana basketball, validation, it seemed, of corn and country values. Plump's shot touched off days of wild celebrations. A convoy of Cadillacs hauled the players around Indianapolis's Monument Circle. Excitement kept the players up most of the night. On Sunday the Caddie caravan headed south down back roads toward Milan. Thousands of people turned out along the way—men waving Indiana and American flags, children perched in the boughs of sycamores, women with freshly baked apple pies and peach cobblers. The parade inched slowly, joyously home. In Milan time had stopped. Hands were shaken, cheers raised, and speeches given. "It's nice to be important," said the coach's wife, "but it's more important to be nice."[32]

Edgar Searcy, an eighth grader at School 17, recalled going to the Senate Avenue YMCA a day or two after Attucks had fallen to Milan. There was the usual amount of good-natured banter and laughter, but at one of the baskets a lone player was dribbling, faking, shooting; dribbling, faking, shooting. He wasn't talking or laughing, just working on his game. It was Oscar Robertson, alone in his own world, lost in the subtle rhythms of the sport. As Searcy scrutinized Oscar, someone intruded into the player's world, razzing him about the Milan game.

"Wait till next year," he said, before returning to his own thoughts.

Chapter Four

"And All We Had to Add Was the Score"

The man drives down country roads, through golden morning light, past grain elevators, cornfields, barns, and churches, scattering autumn leaves, heading toward the town of Hickory, a home he has never seen. At each bend in the road the landscape seems to have sprouted a basketball hoop. Hoops beside grain elevators, hoops nailed to barns, hoops at crossroads. And at every hoop is a scene of quiet activity. This opening sequence of the 1986 film *Hoosiers* presents a powerful scene, touching and full of promise.

It's seductive, this portrait of Indiana in the 1950s. The film praises teamwork and the notion of community. Coach Norman Dale instructs his players to always throw at least four passes before taking a shot, reinforcing the timeless notions of discipline and delayed gratification. The team itself is an extension of the community. Men gather on frosty nights to debate the fine points of man-to-man and zone defenses, and the entire population of Hickory gathers in town-meeting fashion to hold a referendum on the coach. Clearly, the film asserts, little Hickory is the best of America, a place where rural values cling tenaciously.

The city is the lurking evil in this barbershop-quartet world. Represented by South Bend Central, the team the Hickory Huskers confront in the state finals, it is big, loud, ethnic, and, most of all, black. South Bend's players wear newer uniforms than the Hickory Huskers do; they run faster, jump higher, and appear stronger. But the Hickory players are on a mission: "Let's win this one for all the small schools that never had a chance to get here," says one player. On the final shot of the contest, pale-white, square-shouldered Jimmy Chitwood hits a pull-up jumper to win the game for Hickory. The tiny, rural, all-white, small-town team from the rolling south of the state defeats the generic, consolidated, mostly black squad from the northern land of smokestacks.

Hoosiers is, of course, the Hollywood version of the Milan story—quaint, touching, and insidious. Oscar Robertson never saw the film, even though his brother Bailey and high school coach Ray Crowe had small parts. "The team Milan beat, Muncie Central, wasn't all black or anything like it," Oscar recalled. "They had two, maybe three, blacks on the team. But the producers made it a black-white issue. Why? To sell tickets?" As far as he was concerned, *Hoosiers* was *Rocky* on a basketball court—a squad of white, marginally talented athletes led by one star battling uphill against a team of superior players. Beneath the surface, of course, bubbled the subtle, unspoken racism that had always seemed a part of his life.

Hoosiers expresses the racial attitudes of the late twentieth century rather than those of the midcentury. By the last decades of the century, most Americans, white and black, readily accepted the proposition that black athletes were superior to white athletes. "Black is best," wrote S. L. Price in a 1997 *Sports Illustrated* cover story on the decline of white athletes. "That is the under-standing in sports now: not just that blacks are the dominant racial group playing, but also that they possess superior athletic skills and have thus transformed the way sports are played." Bobby Bowden, Florida State football coach, agreed: "An [all-white] foot-ball team in the South in 1960 couldn't touch a football team today that's integrated. Couldn't even touch 'em. You ask what [blacks have] brought to the table? They've brought better athletes."[1]

In the mid-1950s a different ethos governed American perceptions. Black athletes still labored under the long shadow of slavery, and the minds of many whites harbored "Sambo" ste-reotypes of black athletes. Blacks, the argument went, were in-stinctive rather than thoughtful, physical rather than intellectual, complacent rather than ambitious. True, whites viewed blacks as strong, swift, and rhythmic—natural athletic attributes—but such gifts seemed squandered on African Americans. The genetic pre-disposition to play did not, according to the dominant mythol-ogy, prepare blacks to compete in sports because their advantages were offset by a short attention span, low intelligence, infantile dependency, deeply ingrained laziness, and a tropical inclination toward lethargy.[2]

Whites considered blacks inferior in team sports, where raw talent and brute strength ranked below mental acuity, care-ful planning, and coordinated execution. Hit-and-run plays, sac-rifice bunts, full-court presses, line-of-scrimmage audibles, for-mation shifts, diagrammed movements, and memorized playbooks required skills that seemed more natural to white ath-letes. Imagine, the line went, Grambling athletes mastering Knute Rockne's single-wing shift or the New York Cubans perfecting a Tinker-to-Evers-to-Chance double play. Ty Cobb's intensity, Lou

Gehrig's dedication, Joe DiMaggio's dignity seemed beyond the reach of black athletes.

Ultimately, blacks were judged inferior to white athletes, who were viewed as more intelligent, more competitive, and sounder in the basics of a given sport. The speciousness surrounding the mythology of black athletic inferiority was based largely upon the fact that black athletes were invisible. First, whites legally excluded them from big-time professional sports; then, because no blacks played in these contests, whites concluded that blacks were inferior athletes. So powerful was the grip of racism in America that few questioned the logic behind such assumptions.

Of course, things had begun to change. Jackie Robinson had demonstrated beyond any doubt that a black athlete could play intensely, intelligently, and with heroic dignity. Other black athletes had followed Robinson into major league baseball. They chased down long fly balls, pounded home runs out of the park, and blew fastballs past batters. More slowly, they had broken into basketball. In 1950 Earl Lloyd, Chuck Cooper, and Nat "Sweetwater" Clifton became the first three black players in the National Basketball Association, but none of the three became stars. In the mid-1950s black players made more of an impact on the college game. Sherman White at Long Island and Floyd Layne at the City College of New York were outstanding—though both players' careers were cut short by the 1951 point-shaving scandal—and Walter Dukes at Seton Hall was an all-American. Even more impressive were the careers of Bill Russell and K. C. Jones at the University of San Francisco. In 1955, and then again in 1956, the Russell-and-Jones-led Dons used a pressing, shot-blocking, fast-breaking style to capture national championships.

Yet in the mid-1950s, if it was possible to point to a handful of exceptional black basketball players, it was virtually impossible to conceive of an all-black team winning any sort of championship in an integrated tournament. For most of white America, an all-black basketball team conjured one overriding image: five marvelously gifted clowns. By that time the Harlem Globetrotters enjoyed a near monopoly on black basketball talent. Founded in 1927 by businessman Abe Saperstein, the Globetrotters was the most famous sports team in the world. They played games on nearly every continent, from Madison Square Garden and the Boston Garden to cracker-box high school gymnasiums in the Midwest and South to blacktop outdoor courts in South America and Africa. Like Louis Armstrong, the Globetrotter team members had become unofficial ambassadors of the United States, symbols of America's racial harmony, friendliness, and sheer love of a good time. International tours, command performances for royalty, feature movies, and television contracts gave the Globetrotters extraordinary exposure and earned its players the nickname "Clown Princes" of basketball.

The Globetrotters also symbolized something more sinister. The court antics and general demeanor of the players reinforced the very racial stereotypes that athletes like Jackie Robinson battled against. They played the part of Sambo in sweats, prancing around the court, mugging with wide-eyed, toothy smiles, bouncing about like men subject to less gravitational pull. Before a game even started they moved like dancers to the strains of "Sweet Georgia Brown," and their orchestrated stunts continued after tip-off. White audiences loved this basketball minstrel show: Marques Haynes dribbling circles around his hapless white opponents while the rest of the 'Trotters stretched out on the floor like lazy cats feigning sleep; Meadowlark Lemon hiding the basketball underneath his jersey and sneaking down the court to make a basket; Goose Tatum slam-dunking while reading a comic book; all of them cavorting around with deflated, lopsided, or balloon balls, throwing confetti-filled water buckets on indulgent spectators, deviously getting away with every conceivable infraction of the rule book.

It was Uncle Remus meets Amos 'n' Andy, Stepin Fetchit meets Buckwheat—a merry plantation world of dancing bears and toothless tigers. They didn't taunt or scowl, nor did they threaten their white opponents. True, they won their games with remarkable ease, but every white spectator knew that their games were not really *games*. They were . . . well, exhibitions, played against a handful of carefully chosen athletic straight men. Globetrotter opponents fulfilled their duty by delivering the basketball equivalent of straight lines. No straight lines, no jokes. No opponents, no 'Trotter stunts, just one long "Sweet Georgia Brown" circle session.

Abe Saperstein knew what audiences wanted, and he set down the rules for all Globetrotters. Three rules had the authority of commandments: never drive a Cadillac, never contradict a white man, and never, never get caught with a white woman. Saperstein was acutely aware of the fragile nature of the Globetrotters' popularity. White people wanted to see "happy darkies," not "uppity niggers," and Abe sensed that the line between the two was exceedingly fine. He labored to make black athletes into showmen, not gladiators, and he generally succeeded. For most Americans in the 1940s and 1950s, the Harlem Globetrotters epitomized black athletes: hilariously funny, naturally talented, but temperamentally unsuited for real commitment and competition in the big leagues. No white parents ever urged their sons to grow up and be like the Goose or Meadowlark.

Indianapolis was an important part of Saperstein's territory. He owned the Indianapolis Clowns, a barnstorming black baseball team that was part of the rather loose structure of the Negro major leagues. Clowning had always been a controversial part of black baseball. White promoters like Saperstein and Eddie

Gottlieb maintained that clowning attracted spectators, and they encouraged the use of "Deep South Negro" dialects and "happy-go-lucky, lazy fatback-and-grits" stereotypes. Many players, however, argued that clowning degraded their skills and the games. But the fine points of the debate were lost on Saperstein's Clowns. On numerous occasions they painted their bodies to look like African cannibals and took to the field in grass skirts; they adopted such names as Selassie, Mofike, Wahoo, and Tarzan; they slapsticked and jived and shuffled and burlesqued. And, perhaps not surprisingly, they barnstormed into the 1970s, the last of the all-black baseball teams.[3]

Crispus Attucks fed athletic talent to the Clowns and to the Harlem Globetrotters and its satellite teams. Willie Gardner moved directly from Attucks to the Globetrotters, and Cleveland Harp and Hallie Bryant had long careers in the 'Trotter organization. Oscar Robertson's brother Bailey also spent some time with the Globetrotters. After playing competitive basketball in high school and college, they turned showmen for Abe.

Globetrotters and Clowns, racist stereotyping and the near-universal belief in the competitive superiority of white athletes—these were the shadows that haunted black athletes. Jackie Robinson contributed to the Brooklyn Dodgers' 1955 World Series title. Bill Russell contributed to San Francisco's back-to-back NCAA basketball championships. Other black athletes contributed to the success of other professional and amateur teams. But no all-black team had ever won a major title in an integrated tournament in any sport—not at the high school, college, or professional level. Crispus Attucks had come closer than most. In the highly competitive and emotionally charged world of Indiana high school basketball, Attucks had scrambled close to the summit. A few times the school had come close to winning a state crown, so near that its players and fans had gained a palpable sense of what winning it all must be like. But each time something had gone wrong—missed shots, bad calls, errors in judgment—and they had gone home with the bitter taste of another defeat and a dream of next year.

Next year, Oscar Robertson's junior year, bloomed full of hope in the autumn of 1954. Charles Preston, the *Indianapolis Recorder* sportswriter, captured the mood of Attucks supporters: "Pardon us, fellas, if we jump the gun but Ray Crowe has seven veterans back, Willie Merriweather has grown an inch and a half, Oscar Robertson is shooting goals all day long in an alley behind Cornelius avenue—and away we go!" Preston listed seventy-six Attucks students trying out for the team, but all the city's sportswriters agreed that the fifteen-year-old Robertson would be the premier player on the team and in the city.[4]

But other teams in the state seemed to rival Attucks in talent. Muncie Central, the team that lost to Milan in the 1954 state finals, returned a strong team, as did Fort Wayne North and Terre Haute Gerstmeyer. Evansville Lincoln and Gary Roosevelt, two all-black schools, also boasted powerful squads led by outstanding individual players. "All signs point to one of the greatest Indiana high school basketball seasons ever," wrote Preston. And unlike so many previous seasons, Crispus Attucks would get an opportunity to measure itself against the best schools in the state. Where once Attucks had filled its schedule with Catholic and rural schools, now it would play the state's finest teams. Fort Wayne North, Terre Haute Gerstmeyer, Michigan City, and Connersville, as well as all the major Indianapolis schools, were included on its schedule.[5]

Even before Attucks played its first game, 1954 had been a year of improbable events. Marilyn Monroe had married Joe

DiMaggio. Joe McCarthy had withered under the attacks of Army counsel Joseph Welch and journalist Edward R. Murrow. Ho Chi Minh's Vietminh slogged through the mud of Dien Bien Phu on their way to defeating the French in Vietnam. Medical student Roger Bannister broke the four-minute barrier for the mile run. Then less than two weeks after Bannister's mile, another barrier crumbled. By a 9-0 vote, the United States Supreme Court in the case of *Brown* v. *Board of Education of Topeka* struck down the "separate but equal" doctrine in America's public schools. Segregated public schools, the Court affirmed, were "inherently unequal," and they had profound social, cultural, and psychological consequences.

These consequences influenced the North as well as the South, Indianapolis as well as Selma. The facts of the *Brown* case would have seemed sadly familiar to Oscar Robertson. Oliver Brown, a black welder in Topeka, Kansas, brought suit against the board of education because the city's segregated public school system badly inconvenienced his eight-year-old daughter Linda. Rather than attend a white elementary school relatively near home, she had to travel twenty-one blocks to a black school. The long walk took her through a rough part of the city and across dangerous railroad tracks, and it was often made worse by harsh weather. After his mother moved north to Boulevard Place, Oscar's walk to Attucks was almost as long. Sometimes he trudged the twenty-odd blocks on foot, sometimes a friend with a car would pick him up. And all the time, Oscar was aware of the irony that Shortridge High School was only a few blocks east of his mother's house.

He was also aware of another irony. By the start of his junior year, Shortridge administrators, coaches, and students would have certainly welcomed him with open arms. For them, Oscar's grace on the basketball court, composure under pressure, and drive to succeed largely negated his skin color. He could help them be the best team in the city, perhaps in the state. But he had no interest in their conditional acceptance. Crispus Attucks was his school. Its teachers cared about him not as a player but as a person. They never allowed him to believe that basketball was anything more than a means to an end, a way to a better education and a more prosperous life. Years later Robertson recalled the joy in the Attucks halls: "I didn't have to be forced to go to school. I wanted to go. School was an uplifting event. To see your friends, to see teachers that genuinely cared about you—just sitting in class made you feel good."

Edgar Searcy, a teammate of Oscar, had similar memories. Crispus Attucks was the center of the black community, the pride of the neighborhood. It was something pure, untainted by the racism of everyday life, and the blacks in Indianapolis knew it. "It was the rallying point for the whole black community," observed Searcy. "You could go anywhere with your [letter] jacket on. Restaurant owners would say, 'Come on in,' and you would get a good meal. And you never had to worry about a ride anywhere if you had a jacket on."

The centrality of the team to Indianapolis African Americans gave added meaning to winning, the prospects of which appeared excellent for the 1954–55 season. But several tough early-season games would serve as a better yardstick. Attucks was scheduled to open on the road against Fort Wayne North and then play Terre Haute Gerstmeyer eight days later. Two of the highest-ranked teams in the state, they would test Attucks's own elevated ranking.

Hundreds of Attucks fans made the 230-mile round-trip to Fort Wayne, but they seemed lost among the 6,031 people who paid to see the game, part of a doubleheader that also featured Fort Wayne Central battling Marion. Confidently, the Fort

Wayne North Redskins took the court, moved through their pre-game routine, and set up for the opening jump. Their supporters were vocal and partisan. But the confidence and the noise sub-sided dramatically once the contest began. After a minute, Attucks led 6-0. At halftime the lead was 40-28. *Indianapolis Recorder* reporter Charles Preston wrote that Attucks cheerleaders could have started the "Crazy Song" before the end of the second quar-ter, but they delayed their traditional victory celebration cheer.[6]

Reporters were already comparing the 1954–55 Attucks squad, with its 1-0 record, to the best teams in the school's his-tory. Old-timers—who really did not have to be all that old—said it felt like 1951 again, and the talk on the Avenue was that this year Attucks would win it all. Ranked second in the state behind Muncie Central, the Attucks team was for once a subject upon which white reporters for the other three Indianapolis news-papers—the *Star, Times,* and *News*—agreed. Attucks was very good, and junior Oscar Robertson was showing signs of becom-ing the city's finest player.[7]

After crushing rural Sheridan by forty-four points, Attucks opened its "home" schedule in Butler Fieldhouse against a fine Gerstmeyer team. Reporters announced that it was "the game of the year," or at least the first "game of the year." In 1952, and again in 1953, Attucks had gone to Terre Haute to play Gerstmeyer, returning home both times with losses. At the end of both those seasons the Black Cats had advanced to the final four in the state tournament. Gerstmeyer was similar to Attucks in that it drew its athletes from across the city. Players attended Attucks because they were black, regardless of where they lived in Indianapolis. As the technical school in Terre Haute, Gerstmeyer also cast its net broadly. Coach Howard Sharpe welcomed any basketball player in the city who wanted a technical education—and a chance to play in a state championship. If Attucks had hopes of moving to the finals, it had to be able to defeat teams like Gerstmeyer.[8]

In the first half Robertson and his teammates played as if they didn't want to win. Their defense was slack, they made frequent ballhandling errors, and they allowed Gerstmeyer to drag down the game's pace. But the contest was tied at halftime. The pace quickened in the second half. Attucks shifted into a tight press, disrupting Gerstmeyer's patterned offense and forcing repeated turnovers. Sheddrick Mitchell and Willie Merriweather dominated the defensive boards, and Robertson controlled the ball. Gerstmeyer managed only four points in the third quarter as Attucks put the game out of reach. Long before the final whistle, the Attucks stands swayed to the rhythms of the "Crazy Song."[9]

As Gerstmeyer's ponderous, feared offensive movements crumbled under Attucks's in-your-face defense, it seemed as if the old order were passing. Although the Indiana Officials Association continued to reject all applications by African American officials, black players and black teams were altering the tempo of the sport. The year before, across the state line in Illinois, the DuSable Panthers, an all-black squad from the south side of Chicago, had reached the finals of the integrated high school tournament. But their achievements seemed less important than their formula for success. DuSable played high-octane basketball, a pedal-to-the-metal, all-out, all-the-time game. Their weapons were the full-court press, the fast break, and freelance creativity, which they used to humiliate their opponents, averaging eighty points a game in the 1953–54 Chicago high school season. In an age when white high school coaches demanded passing, teamwork, and patience, DuSable players shot almost as soon as the ball touched their hands. In a thirty-two-minute game, they averaged ninety-five shots—a field-goal attempt every twenty seconds. No team—high school, college, or professional—could match their speed in firing the ball at the hoop.[10]

And the Panthers did more than just shoot. They "styled." Decked out in shiny black uniforms, highlighted by long red-and-black knee pads, players with nicknames like "Sweetwater," "Sugar Lump," and "Big Red" and with unusually high numbers on their uniforms turned basketball into a high entertainment form. Instead of a layup line during warm-ups, they formed a dunking line, jumping high and slamming the ball through the hoop. Whether it was the dunking line, the red-and-black knee pads, the fast thirty-foot shots, or perhaps even the sight of Coach Paul Brown's bow tie and lucky plaid vest, a rival coach was moved to observe, "DuSable ain't nothin' but a five-ring circus."[11]

The team may have been a circus, but it was a circus that headed downstate to Champaign for the finals of the state tournament. In the championship game DuSable played Mount Vernon, a school with some seven hundred white and six black students. Of the six African Americans, only one was a male, Albert Avant, regarded as the best athlete in the state. Led by Avant, and aided by a team of friendly referees, Mount Vernon defeated DuSable by six points. In the last four minutes of the game the officials sent two of DuSable's best players to the bench for fouls and waved off four of the Panthers' baskets. But the lesson of DuSable was not lost in the defeat: all-black teams, playing their own brand of ball, could play with and beat any team in their class.

By Robertson's junior year African American players had even begun to have an impact on the game at Indiana University. The week Crispus Attucks blew past Gerstmeyer, the IU varsity players narrowly defeated the IU freshmen. Hallie Bryant was a sophomore on the varsity squad, but two freshmen, Paxton "Sugar Lump" Lumpkin and Charlie Brown of the 1953–54 DuSable team, attracted the most attention. An *Indianapolis Recorder* reporter noted that Bryant had changed his game to fit into the Hoosiers' patterned offense, but Lumpkin and Brown still played DuSable basketball. Brown, "a ball-handling wizard" and long-distance shooter, led the freshman squad with twenty-two points.[12]

Players and students at Crispus Attucks unconsciously sensed, more than they consciously perceived, the quakes in the athletic status quo. Bill Scott, a senior guard on the 1954–55 team, remembered the new mood. "We weren't exactly overconfident, and we weren't exactly cocky, but we knew that we could play with anyone, and we felt like we should win every game." Coach Crowe emphasized the same points: play hard, play smart, keep your head, and you will win.

As the season progressed the players demonstrated their confidence and poise. Not only did they win, they won by large margins. They defeated South Bend Riley by fifteen, Broad Ripple by twenty-eight. Even the spreads were deceiving because Crowe substituted freely, giving all his players a chance. Against South Bend, for example, Robertson scored twenty-eight points, but he watched much of the second half from the bench.[13]

As it had during the previous year, December revolved around the scheduled game with Tech and the city tournament. Even by the standards of Indiana basketball, the interest in the Attucks-Tech game was intense. Both teams swept past their early opponents. Weeks before the game sportswriters speculated about who would win, and 11,255 people crowded into Butler Fieldhouse for the Wednesday-night contest. Never had so many spectators paid to watch a regular-season game, and few left the game feeling cheated. For three quarters Tech maintained a fragile edge, leading by seven at the end of the first quarter, one at the half, and two at the finish of the third quarter. Players threw bad passes and missed open shots, but they also dived for loose balls, hustled on defense, and played with passion. In the fourth quarter the balance of power shifted. Either Attucks increased its pressure defense or Tech wilted, because the Tigers outscored the Greenclads fifteen to three, winning the game by ten points.

The victory clearly established Attucks as the best team in the city, but in their reports of the game several white journalists diminished Attucks's achievement. Unquestionably, some of the slights were neither planned nor intended. Jimmie Angelopolous of the *Indianapolis Times*, for instance, was sometimes criticized for being too openly supportive of Attucks, but even his reports were filled with coded racial messages. Tech was a "well-coached crew" that for most of the contest "outmaneuvered Attucks with a well-planned deliberate offense." Tech "commanded" the lead for three quarters; then Attucks "grabbed" it. The Tigers won, Angelopolous implied, not because they were well coached or played better, but because they were more accustomed to Butler's ninety-four-foot, college-length floor.[14]

Other reporters agreed. "The game probably could be boiled down to this—Tech ran out of gas in the fourth quarter and Attucks kept getting stronger," commented *Indianapolis News* sportswriter Wayne Fuson. It was the court, the ninety-four-foot court, the court that Attucks knew so well, that did Tech in. Tech coach Charlie Maas also blamed the length of the court on his team's slide. He suggested that the next time the two teams met the result might be very different.[15]

The slanted articles bothered Robertson. Beginning in high school and continuing during his college and professional career, white reporters consistently portrayed white athletes as hard working, intelligent, and motivated and black athletes as strong, quick, and physically dominant. "Reporters always wrote that Attucks players were big and strong, but we were no bigger or stronger than many of the other good teams," said Robertson.

"In fact, many times we had a smaller team. And never once, not once, did a white reporter write that I was a smart player. A strong player, yes. A talented player, sure. But not an intelligent player. And intelligence—getting the ball to the right player at the right time, setting up a play, making sure the floor was balanced—was what I did best. But you wouldn't know this by reading the newspapers."

Throughout December and January Attucks continued to win, although not always easily. In the late-December city tournament Attucks breezed past Howe and Washington, only to meet a stubborn Shortridge in the finals. Shortridge shot well from the start, leading by thirteen at the end of the first quarter, four at the half, and three going into the final period. In the last eight minutes of the game Attucks chipped into Shortridge's lead, cutting it to one point in the last half minute. A basket by Robertson gave Attucks the lead, and a free throw by a Shortridge player in the final seconds tied the game.[16]

Both teams made a bucket in the first overtime period, which threw the game into a "sudden death" period. The first team to score would win the game. It was at this crucial point that Ray Crowe silently announced how much faith he had in Oscar Robertson. First he told Robertson to jump center. Although he was three inches shorter than the Shortridge center, he controlled the tip. Then he took the ball and waved his teammates to one side. Herschell Turner, one of the finest guards in the state, played him tight. Oscar began to dribble, faked, drove, pulled up ten feet from the hoop, jumped, and shot. Nothing but net. It seemed so simple, almost as if he could have done it anytime—or every time. No wasted motion, nothing fancy, just a few quick, hard dribbles, a quick, hard stop and jump, and a feather-soft, one-handed shot.

"Throughout the year he'd been asserting himself as the team leader," Crowe later said. "In that game against Shortridge he showed he could back that leadership with clutch play. You cannot imagine what a comfort it was to have such a team-oriented player out on the floor. Oscar made every one of our players just a little bit better, and he had a fierce desire to win."[17]

No one had a better vantage point than Crowe to watch the spectacular development of Robertson. He watched Oscar practice after practice, game after game, watched a fourteen-year-old inconsistent youth mature into a sixteen-year-old veteran who had more patience, consistency, and knowledge of the game than players twice his age. And he had the skill to do what he knew had to be done. Before anybody else, Crowe witnessed it all fall into place. But by early 1955 Indianapolis sportswriters and other coaches saw it as well. Jimmie Angelopolous posed the question in a headline on the *Indianapolis Times* sports page: "Will Oscar Robertson Be Attucks' Greatest?" His answer: yes. Hallie Bryant was a smooth scorer, Willie Gardner a great shot maker. But Oscar had the full package—"temperament, ability, leadership, savvy and team play." Somehow he was able to set up his teammates and still be on pace to break Bryant's single-season scoring record.[18]

With Oscar demonstrating increasing confidence as a playmaker and scorer, Attucks moved into January undefeated and ranked number two in the state. "You could feel it falling into place," remembered guard Bill Scott. They were heady days for Scott. Basketball was more than a sport; it was his salvation, his badge of honor. His family came from the Deep South, from the coal-mining region of Walker County, Alabama, a little out-side of Birmingham. They moved north when the South began to use oil for heating and mines shut down. Scott's mother was already living in Indianapolis with her sister and brother-in-law, so her parents arranged to move there with her son. But before they made the move, Scott's mother was raped and killed. When he finally arrived in Indianapolis with his grandparents in the summer of 1950, his uncle and aunt had converted a garage into living quarters for their relatives.

Scott was dirt poor, and the fact that he lived in a garage did not go unnoticed or unmentioned by his schoolmates. Living in the shadow of California Street, where the wealthier black doctors, lawyers, preachers, and teachers resided, Scott used basketball as a personal social leveler. On the playgrounds of the neighborhood and in the tiny gym at Attucks, he could prove that he was as good, even better, than the sons of the "California Street bourgeoisie." "I wasn't the only one that felt that way," he recalled. "Look at our starting team. We had a lot in common. I was from Alabama. Sheddrick Mitchell and Bill Hampton were from Mississippi. Willie Merriweather and Oscar were from Tennessee. Now it is true that a lot of blacks were moving north at that time, but I also think that we had a little something more to prove. There was a joke that southern blacks told. If you went to Harvester or Ford or Chrysler—the big companies—for a job, don't tell them that you were born in Indy because they know that those people would not work as hard. Those who migrated worked a bit harder so they would be a success and look more prosperous."

The winning streak and the high ranking filled Scott with pride. Life was improving. After two and a half years in the garage, his family had moved into a house at Thirty-fourth Street and Capitol Avenue. For sixty-five dollars he had purchased an old '35 Chevy. "A great car, the kind Al Capone used to drive. Had a window with a shade in the back, and I kept it in perfect condition. Oscar lived just a few blocks away on Thirty-fourth and Boulevard, and I used to pick him up in the mornings and take him to school." With green letter jackets and tall, thin bodies, they stood out like royalty. And they were. "Attucks was our identity," Scott remembered. "It was the focus of the community. For the black community in Indianapolis—even the blacks that did not live around Attucks or even attend Attucks—Attucks basketball was vitally important. Families went to games together, got in cars and drove to away games. In fact, basketball probably kept families together."

During the cold winter the Tigers gave their supporters something to keep them warm. Even when they played poorly they seemed to win. Against Sacred Heart they made only one basket in twenty attempts in the second quarter but still won by nineteen points. Perhaps they were looking ahead to their game against Fort Wayne Central, the third-ranked team in the state. More than eight thousand fans maneuvered their way on ice-glazed roads to watch the game at Butler, and after a slow start Attucks handily won the contest. So it continued. Playing some of the finest teams in the state, the Tigers won with surprising ease. They pounded highly ranked Michigan City by nineteen points. They drubbed Shortridge, looking for revenge for the two-point loss in the city tournament, by thirty-one points. Mishawaka fell by twenty-five points. With Oscar scoring and feeding, and Mitchell and Merriweather dominating the boards, Attucks appeared unbeatable. By the time the team reached 14-0, reporters, fans, and players openly speculated about its chances to finish the season undefeated. "I think the Tigers will become the first undefeated Indiana high school basketball champion in the 44-year history of this Hoosier Madness," wrote Angelopolous.[19]

In late January and early February both the weather and Attucks's fortunes began to chill. After a ten-day layoff the Tigers moved into the most taxing part of their schedule, playing five games in ten days, some against good teams on away courts. Hammond Noll demonstrated that Attucks had weaknesses. Noll was a physical team from the northwestern section of the state, an area known in Indiana as the Region and famous for producing football players. Attucks struggled from the moment the team bus left Indianapolis for the long drive to Hammond. Snow and icy roads slowed traffic and exhausted the players. Hammond's rugged front line and pressing defense also sapped Robertson and his teammates. Bruised and tired, Attucks players entered the last quarter with a ten-point lead and little hope of increasing it. Noll steadily cut into Attucks's advantage. With just over three minutes remaining, Noll captured the lead. With three seconds remaining and the score tied, Billy Brown, a substitute center, hit a free throw, and Attucks escaped the Region with a victory.[20]

Four days and one easy victory later, Attucks faced Connersville in another tough road game. For most of the season Connersville had underachieved, losing six of its sixteen games, but by February its best player had returned to the lineup, and the Spartans were beginning to come together. A Hoosier atmosphere pervaded the Saturday-night game. Connersville's gymnasium, with its low exposed beams and double-decker stands, was crowded with almost two thousand excited spectators. This was the team's chance to salvage a disappointing season by defeating the highly rated all-black squad from the city. So the Connersville faithful were everywhere—packed thick in the stands, wedged in the aisle steps, sitting on the floor in roped-off areas next to the court. When the gym reached its bursting point, latecomers were ushered to the auditorium where they could listen to the game on a WCNB broadcast over school speakers. Outside the temperature registered winter, but inside it was sweaty, shirt-sticking summer hot.[21]

Connersville's gym seemed like a matchbox next to the roomy Butler Fieldhouse. And, in fact, the floor was four feet shorter and three feet narrower than regulation, dimensions that suited the Spartans' zone defense. If Attucks were to win, it would have to win from the outside. For a half, the two teams battled fairly evenly. Attucks briefly held a lead in the first quarter, but by halftime Connersville was up by three. The Spartans played nearly perfectly, hitting a high percentage of their outside shots and occasionally working a backdoor cut for an easy layup. Their fans loved it, cheering wildly—an ocean of clapping hands, stomping feet, and piercing whistles. "Man, it was loud in there," recalled an Attucks player.

Loud and hot. During the halftime break someone decided that everyone else could use some fresh winter air and threw open the outside doors. Inside the gymnasium the hot, humid stationary air mixed with the chilly, moving front and created some freak atmospheric conditions that severely affected the court, which just happened to have been constructed over a swimming pool. By the time the second half began the court was sweating more than the spectators. Charles Preston of the *Indianapolis Recorder* noted that the court resembled "a skating rink" and turned the game into "a farce." One player recalled that there was standing water on the court, which Ray Crowe said was "slicker than glass." "Today they would have stopped the game," said Bill Scott, "but there was no way those officials were going to do anything. Not on their court, and not with them ahead. Too many screaming fans for that to happen."[22]

Reporters white and black later agreed that the slippery court worked to Connersville's advantage by limiting the effectiveness of Attucks's pressing, fast-break brand of basketball. The Spartans played patiently, keeping their feet solid and working the ball slowly. They continued to hit more than 60 percent of the shots they took. By the end of the third quarter they were up by ten, and Attucks was in trouble.

In the final quarter Connersville played a game of cat-and-mouse as Attucks struggled to get back into the contest. In the first half the Spartans had held Robertson to only four points, mostly by preventing him from getting the ball, but in the second half he played more aggressively. Instead of waiting for the ball to come to him, he went out and got it. Somehow he was able to drive toward the hoop, jump, score, and land on his feet without crashing to the floor. He scored eighteen points in the second half, and when the Connersville defense reacted by converging on Oscar, he dealt the ball to Merriweather and Mitchell. In the final quarter Attucks battled the clock as much as Connersville. Oscar had discovered how to win the game, but not necessarily how to win it quickly.

Connersville and the clock won by one point, 58-57. Ray Crowe, as usual, refused to make excuses and was gracious in defeat. The problem was not the officiating, he said, or even the slippery court. "Connersville just outplayed us." Although *Indianapolis Recorder* reporter Charles Preston believed he saw a "twinkle in [Crowe's] eye," no other journalists observed it.[23]

Nor did his players detect the twinkle. They did not have to decode subtle facial variations in their coach or read deeper meanings into his bland public statements. They had failed to perform up to his expectations, disappointing him, their school, and their community, and he let them know it. "We were ashamed to go back to school," Scott remembered. Scott took the loss particularly hard because Crowe singled out poor guard play by Scott and Bill Hampton as the primary reason for Attucks's failure. "I said that wasn't fair to blame me and Hampton. That was a heavy load. I was crying, and he said if I didn't like it, I knew what I could do."

Monday's practice followed the general pattern of a marathon race. A few players recalled that it lasted for almost five hours; others said it lasted longer. Bill Scott harbors a vivid memory of having to run fifty laps. "Mr. Crowe had Johnny Mack Brown lead us. He was . . . a real track guy. Just flat-out fast. Mr. Crowe said that Johnny better not pass anybody. We were all asking Johnny to slow down, but he didn't. And neither did we." Crowe's message was clear: he expected success, and if the starters could not produce, he would find new starters.

With the motivation provided by Crowe's message and Brown's pace, Robertson and his teammates roared into the final phase of the regular season. There were no more icy floors, no more improbable upsets. They beat Indianapolis rivals Cathedral, Manual, and Howe by 43, 20, and 29 points respectively and finished their regular season with a 44-point victory over Bloomington University High School. The wins gave Attucks its most successful regular season. Not only did the team set an Indianapolis single-season scoring record, but Oscar also established a new city individual mark. His 450 points broke Hallie Bryant's 1952–53 record.[24]

Attucks finished so strongly that no Indianapolis sportswriter—and few Indianapolis basketball fans—even entertained the notion that any other city school would remotely challenge Crowe's team. Most writers agreed that Attucks would breeze through the Indianapolis sectional; they disagreed, however, about what would happen next. While some reporters such as Jep Cadou Jr. thought Jasper would win the state title, most journalists favored Attucks or Muncie Central. Throughout the season the two teams had been ranked one and two in the state. Each had stumbled once. In the same week that Connersville had defeated Attucks, Kokomo had beaten Muncie by two points. Both games were widely regarded as flukes, written off to slippery floors, cold weather, and an odd alignment of the stars. When the two powerhouses met—and no one talked about if—state supremacy would be decided.

Bob Collins, one of the leading sportswriters in the city, represented the journalists who felt certain Attucks would defeat Muncie and capture the state title. "Here certainly is the best of Crowe's five Tiger squads," he argued. Attucks had quick guards, quality reserves, and one "great" player, Oscar Robertson. True, the 1951 team with Willie Gardner, Hallie Bryant, and Bob Jewell had better individual players, but Crowe's 1955 players were more aggressive, more unselfish, and better defensively. Most important, they burned with a passion to win. "You can't get this team far enough down to make it quit," Collins wrote.[25]

Of course, Collins had been in the prediction business since 1951 and had never picked a winner. On two previous occasions he had ventured that Attucks would win the state crown, only to face public scorn. As strongly as Collins believed in Attucks, other Indianapolis basketball fans believed there was no way—simply *no* way—that an all-black team could win it all. "For several years," one fan wrote Cadou, "we have had to read you sports writers' stupid articles on how wonderful these Attucks teams are until you get them to believing it." He felt that it was ludicrous to compare Attucks and Muncie Central as if they were equals. "Anybody with an ounce of basketball sense knows Muncie will beat Attucks . . . [by] at least 20 points if they care to pour it on!"[26]

But Attucks supporters did believe, and heady confidence characterized their approach to the Indianapolis sectional tournament. In his presectional story in the weekly *Indianapolis Recorder*, Charles Preston predicted a state title for Attucks, noting, "This is being written, incidentally, BEFORE the Attucks-Washington first-round game, although it will be printed AF-

TER said contest. That doesn't send our blood pressure up a single point. Once this season, we'll confess, we wrote up an Attucks game before it was played—and all we had to add was the score."[27]

Chapter Five

"Out from the Gloomy Past"

So once again it had started, a wish so large that it embraced the entire African American population of Indianapolis. It hardly mattered where blacks lived in the city or where they or their children went to school—Attucks was their team. Each week the *Indianapolis Recorder* was filled with scores of advertisements echoing the same mantra—all the way, Attucks! Win the sectional. Win the regional. Win the semifinal. Win the state. Win all the titles. *We want that crown!* Do it for us. Do it against them. Make us proud. Give us our day.

And once again a few members of the black community decried not so much the optimism as the lack of perspective. At the end of the day, they asked, what did the game accomplish? Observing the passionate interest in basketball in Indiana, *Indianapolis Recorder* editorialist Andrew W. Ramsey wrote, "With all of the preoccupation with the relaxing sport it would seem that Hoosiers would have little time for the American obsession of racism. But unfortunately such is not the case." Basketball, he commented, might make individuals happy or sad; it might give whites a smug sense of superiority or blacks the quick high of putting it to the Man, but what of lasting value did it accomplish? "The Negro who is thrilled by the winning of the team representing his race will emerge from the game to find that he still cannot eat at such and such a restaurant, cannot enjoy the amusements at Riverside Park, cannot work at such and such a job and cannot buy a home outside of the ghetto." Ramsey concluded that the game was "an opiate against the painful experiences of everyday realities along the racial line."[1]

Ramsey was a man of strong opinions and of equally strong loyalties. Charles Preston claimed that Ramsey was an "addict himself," a devoted supporter of the Attucks Tigers. And as far as Preston was concerned, "Mankind can't get through this world we have now without some kind of opiate. Basketball is one of the least harmful varieties." Both Ramsey and Preston joined thousands of other Attucks fans at Butler Fieldhouse for the Indianapolis sectional. They expected several close games, but they also assumed the Tigers would win. Ray Crowe's teams had won three of the previous four sectional tournaments, and they held a 49-4 edge over the other city schools during his tenure as coach. Perhaps, as Preston thought, the only issue left to be decided was by how many points Attucks would win.[2]

It was as easy as that, as easy as Preston thought. Led by Robertson, Attucks dominated its sectional. In its first two games Attucks beat Washington by twenty-eight points and Manual by fifty-one points, advancing to the Saturday semifinal game against Broad Ripple, a team short on talent and long on imagination. Broad Ripple's coach thought that his squad's only chance was to keep the score down by sitting on the ball. Unfortunately for his team, Attucks took a quick lead, and the tactics began to look suspiciously like a desperate attempt not to lose by a lot. Attucks players watched in amazement at Broad Ripple's pointless stall. Soon the watching turned to verbal jousting. With so little playing, there was plenty of time for talking. Bill Scott thought the game was a joke and said as much to his opponents. The idea of not playing to win seemed senseless. Why embarrass themselves in front of thousands of jeering, laughing spectators by standing at midcourt impotently holding the ball and waiting for the final buzzer to signal the end of their humiliation? Broad Ripple's weak reply to Scott's taunts was, "You won't get your averages against us," which was like a boxer celebrating the fact that he got knocked out in the second instead of the first round. "So what?" was Attucks's response. "Play to lose, make it easy on us, give us a chance to rest for the night game." In the end Attucks won 33-19 and was assured of fresh legs for the final game.

Perhaps their restful semifinal contest aided Attucks players in the evening final. At the end of three quarters they were tied with Shortridge, but paced by Oscar's twenty-six points, in the final quarter they coasted to an easy win. In fact, the game was not as close as the 73-59 score indicated. Attucks dominated the boards, made twelve more field goals, and forced repeated turnovers. Long before the final buzzer the Attucks stands rocked to the sound of the "Crazy Song." Oh yeah, the cheerleaders insisted, Washington, Manual, Broad Ripple, and Shortridge were rough and tough—"But they can't beat us."[3]

The Indianapolis regional attracted attention because for the first time since 1951 both Crispus Attucks and Anderson had made it to Butler Fieldhouse. Throughout the week, sportswriters dredged up memories of Attucks's greatest game—the twisting shots by Willie Gardner and Hallie Bryant, the bad calls and missed opportunities, the prayer fling by Flap Robertson, the sound of horns and laughter along Indiana Avenue. It was a moment, they all agreed, to savor and remember. But 1955 was not 1951, and 6' 3½" Oscar Robertson was not 5'9" Bailey Robertson.

Most of the spectators who braved the late-winter blast of snow and rain to watch the regional action sensed that there would be no dramatic rematches. Attucks was the heavy favorite and played with complete confidence, rolling over Wilkinson 95-42 in the afternoon game and then defeating Anderson 76-51 in the finals. Oscar scored on a variety of jump shots, set shots, hooks, and tap-ins and led Attucks with twenty-six points in the first game and thirty-one in the second, but neither his performance nor the victories drew much comment from Crowe. "Well, that's one more step," Crowe told reporters after the game in Attucks's quiet locker room. One more step toward a showdown with Muncie Central and a state title.[4]

"Those games weren't nothing," a longtime Attucks follower remembered. "Wilkinson and Anderson? I had forgotten their names. They might as well have been practice games. Everyone in the state knew that the only game that mattered that year—I mean *the only game*—was Attucks-Muncie." Though residents in other parts of the state might have attached an amendment to that statement, few would have argued with its central thrust. Throughout the year the Muncie Central Bearcats and the Crispus Attucks Tigers had been the top-ranked teams in the state. The year before, Muncie had played Goliath to Milan's David, falling dead when Bobby Plump stopped and popped. The shot that brought so much joy to so many, the basket that defined and validated Indiana's one-class system, showered misery on the rabid Muncie faithful. If there had been a shred of justice in the universe, they contended, Plump's shot would have bounced around the hoop for a suspenseful second or two and then fallen away. Muncie then would have won in overtime and celebrated its fifth state title, and Milan, little Milan, would have limped home saddened but bolstered by the consolation that it had come so close.

It had been Muncie supporters, however, who had to discover some consolation in the loss, and they settled on the fact that all their starters would return for the 1954–55 season. Throughout that year Muncie Central played as if on a mission, rolling over most opponents and stumbling only once in a 65-63 loss to Kokomo. Like Attucks it faced little opposition in its regional, and coaches and experts throughout the state felt the Bearcats would beat Attucks. Wilkinson's coach, Charles Morris, whose team lost to Attucks in regional play, thought coaching would decide the contest. Attucks won, he suggested, because it enjoyed certain physical advantages. "Get a ball club with the physical equipment Attucks has and you'll find the club to beat them. I think Muncie will do it. Taking nothing away from Ray Crowe, but Jay McCreary [Muncie's coach] will probably whip Attucks from the bench. All it's going to take is some good tall boys and some good coaching."[5]

Morris may not have intended to take anything away from Crowe and his team, but he did. His comments and others of a similar ilk suggested that a black coach with an all-black team could not defeat an equally talented all-white or integrated team with a white coach. It hadn't happened before, and the betting line was that it wouldn't happen in Butler Fieldhouse if Attucks and Muncie met in the final game in the semifinal tournament.

On a mild mid-March Saturday afternoon, Crispus Attucks and Muncie Central made sure the "game of the year" would, in fact, take place. In the first afternoon game Attucks took the court against Columbus. The first half of the game was a tight, hard-fought contest, the result, primarily, of Attucks's spotty shooting and frequent turnovers. Early in the second quarter Crowe benched Oscar, sending a message that those in the game better produce. The players grasped his point. By the end of the third quarter the close contest had become a rout. Oscar scored thirteen points in the third quarter, and Attucks scored forty-nine in the second half, finishing with an eighteen-point victory. In the game that followed, Muncie enjoyed similar success, beating Rushville by seventeen points.

After meals and rest the two winning teams returned to Butler for the evening semistate finals. Almost fifteen thousand spectators crowded into the stands and shouted support for their favorite. In a show of urban support, cheerleaders from the other Indianapolis high schools joined the Attucks cheerleaders on the floor. But for once the usual Attucks bravado seemed missing. Muncie's tradition—four state titles, eight appearances in the final game, ten trips to the final four, fourteen times in the round of eight, eighteen contests in the sweet sixteen—inspired near-religious awe among the Hoosier faithful. Its coach had "stepped up" to the post after being the head coach at DePauw University. Its players moved through their pregame drills like seasoned professionals. Its center, 6'6" John Casterlow, cradled the ball high above the basket before dropping it softly through the hoop. Jimmy Barnes, a diminutive guard with a two-handed set shot that he launched from his right hip, swished one after another. Its other starters looked equally ready—stone-faced, intent, serious.[6]

But the Attucks players cared more about current events than about Muncie's storied past. Once the game started they took immediate control. "Play hard, start fast, get a lead, take the refs out of it"—Coach Crowe had given the same advice so many times that he hardly needed to mention it. But he did. And his players responded. "We had a grudge to settle," Attucks guard Bill Hampton said after the game. A grudge not so much against Muncie Central as against the sportswriters who had consistently ranked them second behind Muncie. Attucks hit four of its first five shots and built an 18-9 lead midway through the first quarter, forcing Muncie to call a time-out.[7]

In the second half of the quarter the fortunes of both teams reversed. During the previous week John Casterlow had been feeling poorly. He had played sparingly in the regional tournament, spent Sunday and Monday in bed, and missed most of the week's practices. But suddenly his bout with the "wheezes" seemed to vanish as he grabbed rebounds and put in missed shots. Muncie went on a 14-4 run and finished the quarter leading 23-22.

The shifting dominance that characterized the first quarter disappeared in the second and third as the game became a grim struggle. Ten times the score was tied, and the lead changed fourteen times. But within the wild action a subtle turn was taking place. Simply put: Muncie was having serious problems guarding Oscar Robertson. Gene Flowers was Muncie's best defensive player, and McCreary assigned Oscar to him. But Flowers could not contain Oscar's drives. Several times Oscar faked Flowers out of position and drove past him. The best Flowers could do was recover fast enough to foul him. With two and a half minutes remaining in the second quarter, referees whistled Flowers with his fourth foul, and he spent the third and part of the fourth quarters studying Oscar's moves from the bench.

By the fourth quarter Attucks was also experiencing foul problems. Willie Merriweather, the team's top rebounder, picked up his fourth foul late in the third quarter and went to the bench. He returned midway through the fourth and combined with Oscar to build a 71-65 lead with less than a minute and a half to play. Getting the lead "was as hard as pulling teeth," noted sportswriter Charles Preston, but holding it was even harder. With a minute and twelve seconds left in the game Merriweather hacked Jim Hinds. Merriweather walked slowly to the bench, his evening of basketball concluded. Hinds moved confidently to the free-throw line and made both shots, closing the margin to 71-67. With twenty-nine seconds to play Attucks substitute player Billy Brown fouled John Casterlow, who made his first free throw. His second, however, hit the side of the rim and bounced off to the right, where Gene Flowers tipped it in, cutting Attucks's lead to 71-70.[8]

"The crowd was going crazy, just crazy," Bill Scott remembered. "It was loud and confusing." And Muncie added to the confusion with a wild, scrambling press that trapped Bill Hampton in the corner next to the Attucks stands. "Hampton didn't give up his dribble. He kept it going, just lower and lower," Scott said. "Oscar and I were hollering, 'Pick it up. Give it up. Stick a fork in it.' We wanted him to swing the ball around to one of us. But Hampton's dribble just got lower until there was no dribble left and it rolled out-of-bounds."

Most Attucks fans screamed encouragement, but a few expressed their complete mystification with Hampton's peculiar low-dribbling, Marques Haynes–style ballhandling tactic. Money was at stake on every Attucks game, and the word on the street was that the Attucks-Muncie contest had attracted an unusually high number of bets. "Black dollars and white dollars were riding on the game," remembered an Attucks rooter. "And more than just dollars and paychecks. I know pink slips had been wagered, and I heard that at least one home hung on the outcome." Scott also believed that gambling may have motivated several responses. Like everyone else, he knew about the "business" transacted at the various gambling establishments along Indiana Avenue. Recalling Hampton's turnover, Scott said, "There was a restraining rope between the stands and the court, but one guy was pressing hard against it, yelling at Hampton, 'Man, why did you do that? I should kill you.' He probably thought he was going to lose money on the game."

Muncie had eleven seconds, plenty of time to move the ball down the court for a final shot. Substitute Fred Scott inbounded the ball to Jimmy Barnes, who took a dribble and looked downcourt. At the same moment, Jim Hinds broke for his favorite spot in the corner, and John Casterlow positioned himself under the basket, hoping that if Hinds missed his shot he could tip in the ball. All things considered, it was a fine play, except for one crucial factor: it was exactly the play Robertson expected. Throughout the game he had observed Hinds's tendency to break for the corner; he knew it was the shot Hinds would want and the easiest one to set up. It would simply take too long to work the ball in low to Casterlow, and the Muncie guards had been ineffective all night. So when Hinds broke, Robertson broke in front of him, jumping high to intercept the pass. Then he dribbled toward empty space and just before the final buzzer lofted the ball toward the rafters of Butler Fieldhouse.

"You know," Robertson's friend Bill Swatts recalled decades later, "I've thought about that play a thousand times. Why was it Oscar who made that play? I know why. It was because he never became caught up in the excitement. He never stopped thinking. Everyone else was watching and reacting. Oscar was thinking."

By the time the ball landed, Attucks had begun to celebrate its 71-70 victory. Attucks supporters pushed past the ropes and rushed on the floor, yelling, "All the way!" and trolling for players to hug. Oscar's only concern was getting back to the locker room, but his path was blocked. He had led all scorers with twenty-five points and saved the game with his perfectly timed interception. Now he had to pay the price for his fame. Fans pulled at his jersey and clung to his waist, touching his arms and shoulders and head as if he were a totem. It was a "happy mauling," reported the *Indianapolis Star,* and Oscar didn't really mind. None of the players did. They had just won the biggest game in the history of the school, bigger even than the 1951 Anderson game. In '51 Bailey Robertson had won the game with his loose-wristed, Hail Mary shot. Now another Robertson had done it again, this time with offense and defense.[9]

Once again sports reporters trucked out the superlatives— "the greatest," "the best ever," "an epic contest." They discussed great plays and untimely errors and turning points. "Turning point?" Muncie coach Jay McCreary considered the question during his postgame grilling. "If there was a turning point, it must have been the final buzzer."[10]

Ray Crowe's thoughts were less with turning points than the next week's state finals. His main concern was a massive letdown. All year sportswriters had focused on the Attucks-Muncie game, assuming that that semifinal contest would determine the state champion. But Crowe knew that all the win over Muncie did was make his team eligible for the final day's action. Throughout the week he harped on the point. In 1951 Attucks had gone to the state finals and lost in the afternoon game. The team hadn't been ready, hadn't prepared hard enough, didn't do what needed to get done. Crowe had promised himself that when—he didn't think in "ifs"—his team made it back to the state finals, it would be ready for whatever another team threw at it.

Crowe wasn't the only resident of Indianapolis concerned with preparing for all contingencies. Leading city officials assumed that Attucks would win the state title, and they fretted about what would happen then. Evidently, nightmares of joy-crazed blacks running amuck through white business districts and neighborhoods disturbed them. Early in the week before the championship, Attucks principal Dr. Russell Lane was called into Superintendent of Schools Herman L. Shibler's office, where he had a meeting with his boss as well as a representative of the mayor, the chief of police, the fire chief, and various white business leaders. Lane later summarized the meeting in the crowded office: "The mayor's man said, 'Well, looks like your boys are going to win next week.' I said, 'We think so.' He said, 'We're afraid if they do, your people will break up the city.' I said, 'There will not be one incident.'"[11]

The meeting upset Lane. He knew that the Attucks students and west-side community took pride in the team, celebrated its victories, and lamented its infrequent defeats—but their passions for the Tigers were not destructive. Poor sportsmanship was not a characteristic of either the players, students, or community. Self-control, endurance, respect, and good conduct were cornerstones of Lane's educational and social message. He knew this and so did his "people." But clearly the leaders of white Indianapolis were concerned. The meeting showed how little impact the Attucks basketball team had on some leaders of white Indianapolis. The association between good conduct on the basketball court and good conduct off the court had simply not been made.

But Lane did what he had always done. Repeatedly, he cornered students for "the talk"—be good sportsmen, be good representatives, be good people, and most of all be good. "I told them that if a white student turned over a car in jubilation it would likely be regarded as good-natured foolishness. But if a black student did the same, it could be held against them all as evidence of the Negro's violent nature."[12]

While Lane lectured, Crowe labored to keep his players' minds on the state finals. In order to demonstrate to Indianapolis and the state how well they could handle themselves in victory, they had to win first. One advantage he had was that the racial composition of Attucks's team would not seem such an anomaly. Of the twenty starters on the four teams that had advanced to the Saturday finals—Fort Wayne North, New Albany,

Gary Roosevelt, and Crispus Attucks—thirteen were black and seven white. Of course, Attucks and Roosevelt were all-black schools. Although these numbers went unnoticed or ignored by the Indianapolis daily newspapers, they received headline coverage in the *Indianapolis Recorder*: "The sepia player has come into his own as never before. This is the outstanding feature as the tournament heads for a very probable all-Negro finale."[13]

      With all the talk of the potential firsts—the first Indianapolis state champion, the first all-black state champion, the first all-black state championship game—something did not seem quite right at Crispus Attucks. *Indianapolis Star* sportswriter Bob Collins watched Attucks's practices with a growing sense of concern. Collins was pulling hard for the team, and he was nervous. Ray Crowe was also edgy, carefully gauging every word he said to reporters in a conscious effort to say nothing that would be the least bit provocative or interesting. "We'll be ready," Crowe ventured. "I can't say anything about these boys I haven't said many times before. They started out with one goal—win the state. . . . I said earlier I believed we could do it. I certainly haven't changed my mind." Then, perhaps sensing that he had missed an important cliché, he added, "But we have New Albany next. That's as far as our thinking goes."[14]

      What worried Collins was not Crowe but the players, who seemed oddly relaxed and confident. As they waded through "a battery of photographers" to get to the practice floor, they joked and posed for pictures, taking a singular joy in all the activity buzzing around them. Collins had been to other such sessions, and he had come to expect grim-faced, laconic athletes who looked as if they were about to be the guests of honor at a public execution. Instead, between photo sessions the Attucks players fired random shots at the hoop and smiled at everyone and everything. Their attitude was contagious, and soon even Collins relaxed and enjoyed the show.

Collins correctly sensed the source of their mood. While not exactly overconfident, Robertson and his teammates believed that the other three teams in the tournament had more to worry about than they did. Attucks had defeated the top-ranked team in the state, the team most reporters expected to win it all. And although New Albany, Attucks's afternoon opponent, had been running up the score against other teams, the looks on Crowe's players' faces seemed to say, "We know they can't score like that against us."[15]

On Saturday morning, March 19, the temperature was just below freezing, but by noon it had climbed into the high forties. A light drizzle and a gray sky, however, made it feel colder. Yet few Attucks supporters took much note of the outside conditions; it would be hot, stuffy, and loud inside Butler Fieldhouse. Attucks played New Albany in the first game, so the traffic from the city's west side began to snake north toward Butler long before tip-off time. It inched over Fall Creek, near Robertson's home on Boulevard, past Crown Hill Cemetery, to the barnlike fieldhouse just off Forty-ninth Street. One Attucks fan recalled that the automobiles, decked out in Attucks gold and green and displaying signs of support, looked and sounded like "a circus coming into town."

If the Attucks players had enjoyed a remarkable serenity during the week leading to the championship tournament, they displayed youthful jitters once their afternoon game began. Collins said they were "drum-tight." Rather than protecting the ball, they treated it as if it were something to get rid of as fast as humanly possible. In the first half alone they self-destructed seven times on three-on-one or two-on-one fast-break opportunities, either by throwing bad passes or forgetting to dribble before they ran. And when they did not commit turnovers they arched ill-considered shots. Fortunately, New Albany was just as tight and considerably less talented.[16]

For three quarters the game was a contest of spurts. Attucks would build a lead, then New Albany's outstanding guard Jim Henry would close it. For a few moments in the second quarter New Albany even crept into the lead. But gradually Attucks's quickness and rebounding superiority wore down New Albany. In the fourth quarter the southern team mounted one last charge, cutting the score to 65-58 with six minutes and twenty-five seconds to play. Then, in thirty seconds, Robertson scored two field goals and two free throws to put the game out of reach, and Attucks coasted to a 79-67 victory. These Tigers had done what the 1951 team had failed to accomplish: earn a spot in the championship game.

The second afternoon game between Fort Wayne North and Gary Roosevelt was more competitive. Like Crispus Attucks, the all-black Roosevelt team was loaded with talent. Wilson Eison, the finest center in the state, would later be chosen as Mr. Basketball in Indiana for 1955 and go on to Purdue University and all–Big Ten honors. And forward Dick Barnett would later lead Tennessee State to several National Association of Intercollegiate Athletics titles and play for more than a decade in the NBA. Not knowing the future, however, Fort Wayne assumed it had a fair chance to win the game.

For a quarter the two teams played evenly; then Roosevelt mounted a 16-0 run, leading Fort Wayne by eleven points at the half. Midway through the fourth quarter Roosevelt led by six-teen points, and the game seemed out of reach. Then the two coaches made key decisions. Roosevelt's coach told his team to stall, a move that effectively muzzled Eison and Barnett. Fort Wayne's coach sent his 6'10" center to the bench and instructed his team to go into a full-court press. The press worked. The stall didn't. In five minutes Fort Wayne outscored Roosevelt 16-2 but fell two points short of sending the contest into overtime. Roosevelt survived the game tired and convinced that stalling was not a particularly good idea, two factors that would benefit Attucks.

That night almost fifteen thousand spectators jammed Butler Fieldhouse. But Bill Scott remembered that except for the hard-core fans from Attucks and Roosevelt it was an oddly quiet crowd. The reason was obvious. Neither team had a single white player. Never before had anyone seen anything quite like the scene on the court. Spectators watched black players, black coaches, and black student managers prepare for the contest, and if white cheerleaders from the other Indianapolis and Gary schools had not joined the Attucks and Roosevelt cheerleaders in respective demonstrations of city unity, there would have been only black cheerleaders as well. For many white Indiana basketball fans, it almost seemed as if their game had been kidnapped. On the same night that Bill Russell and K. C. Jones shattered racial stereotypes by leading the University of San Francisco to an NCAA title in Kansas City, taboos about race also crumbled in Indianapolis.

Exactly how much race mattered—and what precisely the game meant in racial terms—would later spark lively debates along Indiana Avenue and in the pages of the *Indianapolis Recorder*. Charles Preston claimed that race was not an issue. To be sure, he overheard racially motivated comments. One white "liberal" said, "I hope two Negro teams don't go to the final game—it will make the white people mad." And a white cashier in a store with a large black clientele added that she hoped Attucks lost because "there'd be no livin' with 'em" if the west-side team won. Who the "'em" was went unsaid but was understood.[17]

Still, Preston maintained, such incidents were isolated, lonely cries of bitterness among a larger consensus of acceptance. Mayor Alex M. Clark, downtown merchants, and students of the other Indianapolis schools supported Attucks in a color-blind fashion. Another *Recorder* editorialist agreed: "We would not deny that a small minority of crackpots continue to hate along racial lines. Yet all reliable signs show that the question of color was not in the minds of most fans." This writer felt that whites who cheered against Attucks probably did so not because of race but simply out of an impulse to support the underdog, just as many Americans rooted against the New York Yankees.[18]

Andrew W. Ramsey, however, offered a less benign interpretation of the crowd. Both before and during the game he heard racial epithets, most uttered carelessly and unthinkingly. But he was less interested in how people behaved during the game than what the contest meant. On one level the racial composition of the finals exploded racial myths and stereotypes:

> The appearance of two Negro teams in the final game struck at the vitals of the myth of the inherent inferiority of the Negro and belied the calamity howlers who in 1941 predicted that if Negro schools were admitted to the then lily-white Indiana High School Athletic Association, race riots would follow. It also undermined the myth that explained the stellar performance of Negro athletes on integrated school teams but denied the possibility of a Negro-coached team ever excelling—the myth that Negroes need the guidance of a white man in order to accomplish anything great.

But at a deeper, more profound level, the game underscored not racial progress, but the lack of it. "The very existence of three all-Negro schools in Indiana is a denial of the democracy that Attucks and Roosevelt's appearance in the final game affirmed," Ramsey wrote. Several Indianapolis blacks who had fought the good fight to get Attucks into the IHSAA watched the game with mixed emotions, proud that two black high schools had won the right to play in the final game, but with vague misgivings about the future. Thoughts of "what next and when" now occupied their minds.[19]

In the stands there may have been time for rumination. On the court all that mattered was the game. Once it began, even the neutral spectators became vocal. "I think a lot of white people started to cheer for us because Roosevelt's uniforms made them look like the Harlem Globetrotters," remarked Scott. "And we started so fast it made it easy to root for us."

From the opening tip the game belonged to Robertson. He jumped center, won the tip against the taller Wilson Eison, got the ball back at the top of the key, made a quick fake and a hard dribble, pulled up, and hit a sixteen-foot jump shot. The game was only eleven seconds old, but if one play could constitute a pattern, this one did. It was not that any single part of it was remarkable. The fake, the dribble, the shot—all were the sort thousands of players had performed hundreds of thousands of times. What was singular was how easy he made it look. The Roosevelt defender looked like a child covering a man. He was there, but he was helpless against the brutal economy of Oscar's game.

Repeatedly, Robertson worked variations of the same basic moves. Sometimes he faked and shot without dribbling. Other times he just took a quick dribble or two and shot. Or he took a dribble, hesitated, sensed an opening, and drove in for a layup or was fouled. Often he faked left, drove down the right side of the six-foot lane, and squared up for a short jumper. Then when Roosevelt began to double- or triple-team him, Robertson made sharp, no-frills passes to an open teammate. Roosevelt just did not have a defense to stop Oscar Robertson.

Led by Robertson, Attucks's players applied constant pressure. On defense they pressed full-court and challenged every pass. On offense they pushed the ball up the court and took the first open shot. No four or five passes, then looking for the shot; no walking the ball up the court. Just constant offensive and defensive pressure. "That was our game plan," Robertson recalled. "We knew that if we could play up-tempo they could not stay with us." Roosevelt couldn't. Instead of trying to slow down the game, many of the Roosevelt players attempted to do too much. Eison was effective around the basket, but his teammates often played as if there were only three seconds left on the clock and they were down by a point. They forced passes, lost control of their dribbles, and flung Hail Mary shots. A few went in. Most didn't. Although Eison could not keep his team in the game or even make it respectable, he was able to prevent a complete embarrassment.

But the game was never in doubt. Attucks led 24-15 at the end of the first quarter, then connected on nine of twelve shots in the second quarter to take a 51-32 lead at the half. Fifty-one points in a sixteen-minute half of a championship game was like running a four-minute mile in a high school meet. It stunned Indianapolis sportswriters who thought they had seen it all. Bob Collins of the *Star* wrote that "the magnificent Tigers of Crispus Attucks" "awed" spectators and opponents alike. "The first quarter was only half over when the Panthers began looking like fighters who had been caught with that one punch too many."[20]

With the outcome of the game settled by the end of the first half, the television announcer and spectators found other questions to occupy their interest. Would Attucks score a hundred points? Would Robertson break the record for the most individual points scored in the semifinals and finals? As Attucks approached the century mark, cheering increased, but in the end the team fell three points short, winning the game 97-74. Robertson did break by four points the old individual scoring record of ninety-one. Unfortunately, Eison also broke the record, scoring two more points than Robertson. On the last play of the game Robertson had an opportunity to tie Eison. He drove toward the basket and had an open shot but passed the ball to Willie Burnley, a senior reserve who was positioned under the basket. For several sportswriters, Robertson's unselfish pass was as important as his thirty points.

Then it started, a celebration that had been building for years. In the forty-five years of the Indiana state basketball tournament, it was the first victory by an Indianapolis school, and Mayor Clark was more than willing to tell anyone who would listen that the long city nightmare had ended. Crispus Attucks— *Indianapolis* Crispus Attucks, as he liked to say—was the new state champion.

But the victory did not really belong to the city, as Clark must have known. If it had, why was there a need to bolster the normal police details in the city? Why had so many detectives been assigned to Butler Fieldhouse? Why had city officials worried about civil disturbances? Why had there been so much talk about race? In a city where the races were largely separate and unequal, where blacks were simply not free to enter many stores, theaters, and restaurants, how could the races come together and celebrate? And if something happened—a remark, an embrace, a knowing look—what then? "We really didn't know what was going to happen," Clark later admitted. "Those police were a booster shot."[21]

The victory belonged to black Indianapolis, and whites and blacks knew it. In the black community the victory far transcended what had happened on the court, and its meaning was epic. The lead editorialist in the *Indianapolis Recorder* set the tone, beginning with a quote from Matthew: "The stone which the builders rejected is become the head of the corner." Continuing the biblical theme, the writer asserted:

> It is with a spirit of profound reverence and thanksgiving that we hail the new high school basketball champions of Indiana, the Crispus Attucks Tigers. Persons unfamiliar with our state may believe that we are overdoing it in going down on our knees and giving praise to Almighty God that this glorious thing has come to pass. But basketball—especially the high school variety—occupies a peculiarly lofty place in the Hoosier scheme of things. It is far more than a boys' sport—in fact, [it] is just about the most important thing there is.

Moving from sacred to secular, the editorialist ended with a passage from James Weldon Johnson's "Lift Ev'ry Voice and Sing":

> *Stony the road we trod,*
> *Bitter the chastening rod*
> *Felt in the days when hope unborn had died;*
> *Yet with a steady beat*

Have not our weary feet
Come to the place for which our fathers sighed?
We have come over a way that with tears has been watered;
We have come treading our path through the blood of the
    slaughtered,
Out from the gloomy past,
Till now we stand at last
Where the white gleam of our bright star is cast.[22]

The explosion of pure joy and the meaning of the victory can only be interpreted in such powerful terms. For a community and a population that had had little reason for mass celebration, the victory inspired many to invoke biblical stories and liberation poetry. "Man, it was sweet," recalled an Attucks fan who was at the game. "Smiles everywhere—everywhere. And tears, too. Oh, yes. Plenty of tears. I personally hugged two people I disliked and every friend I could find. It was something."

After an extended period of whooping and hollering and embracing, the players showered and dressed and departed Butler on top of a red fire truck for the traditional "glory ride." It was a cold night, but few noticed. Slowly their truck, led by Mayor Clark's limousine and a detail of police motorcycles and followed by a long line of automobiles and buses, moved east on Forty-ninth Street and south on Meridian Street toward Monument Circle, the centerpiece of Indianapolis. Meridian was lined with people—most cheering, others just watching from the lawns of their big houses. At Monument Circle the truck made a victory lap around the fountains, statues, and shaft dedicated to Indiana Civil War veterans. It moved past the limestone soldiers, beardless and eternally youthful, past the crowning figure of *Victory*, known for more than half a century as simply *Miss Indiana*, past the other memorials in bronze and stone. The truck made a quick stop at the Circle while the mayor presented the key to the city to Coach Crowe, then it veered northwest along Indiana Avenue and north on West Street, past Crispus Attucks, to Northwestern Park. There in the city's black section the truck stopped and the real celebrations began.[23]

A large bonfire illuminated the park and the crowd of twenty-five thousand cheering Attucks supporters. As the players scrambled off the truck they were treated like gods: Bill Scott and Bill Hampton, who scored only six points each but played tenacious defense against Roosevelt's guards; Sheddrick Mitchell and Willie Merriweather, who contributed eighteen and twenty-one points respectively and helped Attucks win the battle of the boards; and Robertson, most of all Robertson, who led Attucks with thirty points but whose play was so much more important than any final tabulation of points, assists, and rebounds. They were all cheered again and again. They were hugged and patted; their backs were slapped and their hands shaken. And for most it felt great. Scott recalled the pure joy of celebrating with "his people" in "his neighborhood": "There was no place I would have rather been that night, and no people I would have rather been with. I was just so happy."

Bill Swatts, a friend and classmate of the players, felt the same way. "I thought that the bonfire was great. I didn't think then that the white kids got to get off their fire trucks at the Circle and had a big party, but that we were taken to a segregated area for our celebration. I guess the powers that be thought that we would tear up the downtown if we had had our party there. But at the time that thought never crossed my mind. Oscar thought about it, though. He was always perceptive, and that was one of the reasons I respected his intelligence."

Oscar felt—and continues to feel—that the celebration at Northwestern Park was a slap in the face:

When Milan won the state championship they got a ride around all the squares in Indy—all through the downtown. But when it was an all-black school with ten or twelve black players, city officials thought that all these black people would terrorize the city. "We can't have them congregating around our Circle monument," they probably said. "We will take them back to their neighborhood." And the police escorted us there.

I will never forgive them for it myself. I try, but I can't. We were not savages. Our skins happened to be black. But we didn't tear up things; we didn't rob people. We didn't do those things. We were civilized, intelligent young people who through the grace of God happened to get together and win some basketball games. Then we won the biggest game in the history of Indianapolis basketball, and they took it away from us. How can you forgive them for doing that, for snatching our innocence? I will never forgive them. I can't even get my mouth to form the verb.

Robertson turned his back on the bonfire and celebration while the festivities were still in full swing and caught a ride back to his father's house. For a teenager who had just lived every Hoosier schoolboy's dream, he didn't feel so great. When he got to the house he was quiet and pensive. "I'm tired of all that noise," he told his father. Always hungry, he made a sandwich, then stretched out on the living-room floor and began to watch television. His father studied Oscar, knowing something was wrong but not asking any questions. "Oscar was quiet," Bailey Robertson Sr. remembered. "Finally he said something like, 'Dad, they don't like us, do they?'" But he wasn't looking for any answers or discussions. "He just pulled himself up and went to bed."

The victory had temporarily united Indianapolis, but the celebrations exposed its fault lines. In the week that followed the contest, one fact became painfully clear to Indianapolis blacks: city officials were happy that Attucks had ended Indianapolis's forty-five-year drought, but that did not mean they wanted any downtown celebrations. Reporters and nearly all Attucks fans expected the city to spring for a parade. It seemed only right. After all, Roosevelt had lost, but Gary officials had still staged a five-mile parade to city hall before forty thousand fans. And just as many fans wanted an even more grand demonstration for their local heroes. But Mayor Clark and his advisers decided that the "Big Parade" idea was a bad idea. What was a good idea was to follow the Northwestern Park celebration with another celebration inside the black community.

On the Thursday following the game, Mayor Clark, city officials, chamber of commerce leaders, and representatives of the Downtown Merchants Association made the short drive to Crispus Attucks to honor the school and the team with a resolution, a plaque, the promise of a scholarship fund, and an assortment of speeches. It was a sedate affair, quite different from the previous Monday's joyous celebration at Crispus Attucks. "Whether all this can adequately substitute for the anticipated Downtown Parade and/or City-Wide Banquet is a question for the fan in the street to determine," a *Recorder* reporter wrote.[24]

It couldn't and it didn't. Robertson and the other players knew that the meals they ate on the "rubber-chicken circuit" and the talks they heard about how important they were to the city did not satisfy the Indianapolis black community, which ached for a massive, integrated, public celebration in the heart of the city. Hundreds of people phoned Crispus Attucks and the offices of the *Recorder* to vent their anger. Perhaps, as one editorialist

*C*rispus Attucks High School shortly after its founding in 1927. Built to segregate Indianapolis's black high school students, it was often overcrowded and under-funded. Despite the obstacles, its dedicated staff provided students with quality education. Crispus Attucks survives today as a middle school.

Indiana Historical Society, Bass Photo Co. Collection 209526F

*D*r. Russell Lane taught English at Crispus Attucks when it opened and then served as the school's principal from 1930 to 1957.

Indiana Historical Society, Indianapolis Recorder Collection C7252

*T*he Indiana High School Athletic Association held the state finals in Butler Fieldhouse (now Hinkle Fieldhouse) from 1928 to 1942 and from 1946 to 1971. The fieldhouse is reputedly the nation's oldest basketball arena. *Indiana Historical Society, Bass Photo Co. Collection 267604F3*

*R*ay Crowe first served as head basketball coach at Crispus Attucks during the 1950-51 season. Members of that season's team were (left to right) Charles Cook, Pervis Henderson, Benny Cook, Dejuain Boyd, Hallie Bryant, John "Noon" Davis, Charles West, Larry O'Banion, Charles "T" Toliver, William Mitchell, Bailey Robertson, and Stanley Warren. Not pictured are Leahman Covington, Willie Gardner, and Bob Jewell.

Frank Fisse photograph, courtesy Stanley Warren

"But They Can't Beat Us"
Oscar Robertson and the Crispus Attucks Tigers

On March 16, 1951, the day before the state finals, Attucks students paraded down Indiana Avenue to show support for their team. These students were riding a nautical-themed float sponsored by Kingan and Company. So many students jumped onboard, according to the **Indianapolis Star**, that the float's rear tires blew; and the students were forced to "abandon ship and take to the lifeboats."

*Indiana Historical Society, **Indianapolis Recorder** Collection C7858*

The 1950-51 Crispus Attucks basketball team celebrates its 1951 regional win over Anderson.
Courtesy Ray Crowe

*T*he Tigers hoist Coach Ray Crowe in the air after defeating Arsenal Technical High School in the 1954 Indianapolis sectional. Oscar Robertson is second from left; at far right stands Assistant Coach Al Spurlock.

Courtesy Frank Fisse

*D*on Layton of Indianapolis Howe attempts to steal the ball from Oscar Robertson during city-tourney action at Butler Fieldhouse, December 29, 1954.

Courtesy Frank Fisse

"But They Can't Beat Us"
Oscar Robertson and the Crispus Attucks Tigers

*O*scar Robertson drives around Fort Wayne Central's Dave Shearer in a January 12, 1955, game at Butler.

Courtesy Frank Fisse

*C*rispus Attucks fans show support for their team in a game against Indianapolis Shortridge on January 18, 1955.

Indiana Historical Society, ***Indianapolis Recorder*** *Collection C7899*

*R*ay Crowe huddles with his 1954-55 starters (left to right): Oscar Robertson, Sheddrick Mitchell, Willie Merriweather, Bill Hampton, and Bill Scott.

Courtesy Indiana Basketball Hall of Fame

*M*axine Stantley receives cheerleading help from a small friend, Ramona Oglesby, during the 1955 Indianapolis sectional.

Indiana Historical Society, **Indianapolis Recorder** *Collection C7848*

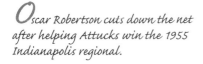

*T*he champions of the 1955 Indianapolis sectional celebrate on the floor of Butler Fieldhouse.

Courtesy Frank Fisse

*O*scar Robertson cuts down the net after helping Attucks win the 1955 Indianapolis regional.

*Indiana Historical Society, **Indianapolis Recorder** Collection C7222*

"But They Can't Beat Us"
Oscar Robertson and the Crispus Attucks Tigers

*A*lonzo Watford, Attucks's athletic director, ponders the best method for distributing tickets for the 1955 state finals. After students, teachers, and the players' families received theirs, few of the 1,013 tickets allotted to Attucks remained for the general public. According to the **Indianapolis Recorder**, school administrators "tried to distribute the precious pasteboards on a fair basis."

Indiana Historical Society,
Indianapolis Recorder *Collection C7248*

*T*he 1954-55 team gathers in the locker room. Front row: Johnny Mack Brown, Stanford Patton, Bill Brown, Oscar Robertson, and Sam Milton. Back row: Coach Ray Crowe, Willie Burnley, Bill Hampton, Willie Merriweather, unidentified manager, Bill Scott, and Sheddrick Mitchell.

Courtesy Frank Fisse

A more official shot of the 1955 state champions. Front row: Stanford Patton, Sam Milton, Bill Hampton, Bill Brown, Bill Scott, and Johnny Mack Brown. Back row: Coach Ray Crowe, Willie Merriweather, John Gipson, Oscar Robertson, Sheddrick Mitchell, and Willie Burnley.

Indiana Historical Society, **Indianapolis Recorder** *Collection C7223*

*T*he Crispus Attucks track team, circa 1955. Al Spurlock (center, back row) coached several of his basketball players in track and field. Included in this picture are Johnny Mack Brown (third from left, front row) and Willie Merriweather, Henry Robertson, and Oscar Robertson (first, second, and fifth from left, respectively, in the back row).

Indiana Historical Society, **Indianapolis Recorder** *Collection C7236*

The program for the 1956 state finals featured photographs from the previous year's tournament. In the center of the program is a picture of Oscar Robertson and Willie Merriweather receiving the 1955 winner's trophy from Otton Albright, IHSAA president.

*Indiana Historical Society, **Indianapolis Recorder** Collection KCT270*

Oscar Robertson, Ray Crowe, and Albert Maxey in 1956.

Courtesy Frank Fisse

*A*ttucks supporters cheer their team to victory over Cathedral in the 1956 Indianapolis sectional.

*Indiana Historical Society, **Indianapolis Recorder** Collection C7869*

*T*he Tigers enjoy their second-straight state championship, March 17, 1956. The 1955-56 Tigers were the first unbeaten team to win the state title, though they did not hold that exclusive honor for long. The 1957 champion, South Bend Central, also went undefeated. *Courtesy Frank Fisse*

The 1956 titleholders. Front row: Henry Robertson, Bill Brown, Lavern Benson, Albert Maxey, and Sam Milton. Back row: Assistant Coach Al Spurlock, Edgar Searcy, Odell Donel, Oscar Robertson, Stanford Patton, James Enoch, and Coach Ray Crowe.

Courtesy Frank Fisse

Oscar Robertson escorts Ramona Reeves to Iota Phi Lambda sorority's debutante ball, May 1956. Reeves was chosen debutante queen.

Indiana Historical Society, **Indianapolis Recorder** *Collection C7230*

Indiana Avenue in May 1956, the spring Crispus Attucks won its second-straight basketball championship. At the end of the street is the Walker Theatre, an Indianapolis landmark since 1927.

Indiana Historical Society C7865

"BUT THEY CAN'T BEAT US"
OSCAR ROBERTSON AND THE CRISPUS ATTUCKS TIGERS

By the 1950s the Indiana Avenue neighborhood was declining, but it was still the heart of Indianapolis's African American community, and it was home to many mom-and-pop businesses such as Winston's Store.
Indiana Historical Society C7867

"But They Can't Beat Us"
Oscar Robertson and the Crispus Attucks Tigers

*T*hough the Tigers received an official championship trophy from the IHSAA, the **Indianapolis Recorder** collected money from the community to help pay for an additional one. This trophy, presented to the team in June 1956, featured the ball used in the championship game as well as the shoes the players wore—all plated in bronze. Receiving the trophy are (left to right) Stanford Patton, Bill Brown, Albert Maxey, Sam Milton, Odell Donel, Henry Robertson, James Enoch, Edgar Searcy, Lavern Benson, and Coach Ray Crowe.

Indiana Historical Society, **Indianapolis Recorder** Collection C7851

*T*he **Recorder** also gave each of the 1956 championship players one of his shoes plated in bronze. Here, George J. Thompson, business manager of the paper (standing at right), presents the individual trophies to (left to right) Henry Robertson, Bill Brown, Coach Ray Crowe, Edgar Searcy, Oscar Robertson, and Assistant Coach Al Spurlock.

Indiana Historical Society, **Indianapolis Recorder** Collection C7224

*O*scar Robertson, Indiana's Mr. Basketball, takes on Kelly Coleman of Kentucky during practice for the Indiana-Kentucky Blind Fund Classic, better known as the all-star game, June 1956.

Courtesy Frank Fisse

*F*uture University of Cincinnati basketball star Oscar Robertson greets former University of San Francisco star Bill Russell at Butler Fieldhouse, October 25, 1956. Russell was a member of the U.S. Olympic basketball team, which was on a fund-raising tour.

Indiana Historical Society, **Indianapolis Recorder** *Collection C7228*

"But They Can't Beat Us"

Oscar Robertson and the Crispus Attucks Tigers

The success of the Crispus Attucks basketball teams inspired future generations. In pickup games on courts throughout Indianapolis's black neighborhoods, young players worked to improve their skills, dreaming of one day becoming champions themselves.

Indiana Historical Society, **Indianapolis Recorder** Collection C7856 commented, Indianapolis was simply "undemonstrative." Perhaps. "But the circumstance of the city's first state champs' happening to be a Negro team, and the possibility of misunderstanding that the 'no parade' decision might be somehow connected with that circumstance, perhaps could have influenced the city fathers to sing, along wi[t]h the rest of us, 'I Love a Parade.'"[25]

Though the issue remained hot, there never was a parade. No matter, said some, the championship was enough. But for others, Robertson included, it wasn't. Though he was not particularly fond of public celebrations of any sort, he knew, even then, that the absence of one was a powerful expression of the racial order in Indianapolis.

Chapter Six

GIANT STEPS

Few, if any, of the reporters who covered Indiana high school basketball noticed the sad irony of white coaches and administrators singling out Crispus Attucks as a recipient of an odd kind of favoritism. White Indianapolis politicians had founded the school so that their children and the children of their constituents would not have to attend high school with black pupils. The same politicians had consciously and consistently underbudgeted Attucks and then joined with other white officials in the state to keep Attucks and other black high schools out of the Indiana High School Athletic Association.

Against this coalition of politics and racism, however, Attucks quietly fought back. The school's administrators—all black—took the meager budget scraps parceled out by the state and created a banquet. They staffed and ran a school that was the pride of the community, lobbied and petitioned for admittance into the IHSAA, and battled to overcome racial notions of athletic superiority and biased officials just to compete in basketball games. Then, after the years of rejection, frustration, defeat, and pain; after the snubs, jeers, taunts, and slurs; then, they watched their team—their all-black Crispus Attucks Tigers—win the Indiana state basketball championship. And they celebrated, shaking hands and slapping palms while the flames from a bonfire climbed high into the chilly night above Northwestern Park.

But soon after the championship a whispering campaign took hold. "Of course Attucks won," went the new party line. "Lord knows, they had every advantage. Not only did they recruit from across the city, they got an added home-court advantage." That was the delicious irony. Although every white high school in Indianapolis had a fine gymnasium, Attucks's gym was barely adequate for physical education classes and certainly incapable of seating thousands of Tiger rooters. Throughout the early 1950s Attucks administrators tried to get the funding for a new gym. They failed. The *Indianapolis Recorder* printed editorial after editorial demanding the simple justice of a decent gym for Attucks to permit home games. They were not asking for the best gym in the state; that would be tantamount to asking for the moon. It did not even have to be the best in the city—just good enough. But the editorial pleas failed to move anyone with the power to make a difference. So Crispus Attucks basketball players became a roving band of gifted athletes, a team without a home. To make up for this peculiar disadvantage, they scheduled their "home" games in the gymnasiums of other city schools. Sometimes they played at Tech, whose 4,500-seat gym could hold most of the Attucks faithful. More often they played at Butler Fieldhouse, a cavernous facility that could seat 15,000.

Butler suited Attucks fine, though it occasionally created scheduling problems. Sometimes Attucks would not play a game for a week or ten days, then have to play three games in four days. But the demand for Attucks tickets and Butler's size compensated for the scheduling difficulties. Twice during the previous regular season more than eleven thousand people had paid to see important Attucks games against Tech and Shortridge. Butler made money from the deal, as did the IHSAA. Attucks also showed a small profit. Since no new gymnasium had been built at Attucks during the summer of 1955, school officials again scheduled the "home" games away from home. Initially, Attucks planned to play sixteen of its regularly scheduled games in Butler Fieldhouse.[1]

That was when the problems started. Attucks's plans, it seemed, did not meet the approval of other coaches and athletic directors. In August the high school coaches held their regular meeting at Purdue University, and a handful complained about the Attucks schedule, suggesting it gave the Tigers an "unfair" advantage. Given the fact that the city and state tournaments would once again be held at Butler, Attucks would have a "special" knowledge of the court. IHSAA commissioner L. V. Phillips told an *Indianapolis Recorder* reporter that he was "sympathetic" to Attucks's difficulty. "I think the majority of coaches understand the problem and are tolerant," he added. But the same tolerant coaches still felt, sadly, that the salient fact was that Attucks spent too much time on Butler's court.[2]

Phillips explained to reporters that the complaints he heard were not personal. In fact, they hardly even rose to the level of complaints, just sort of off-hand remarks that Phillips did not take before his Board of Control. "They were wholly unofficial," the commissioner emphasized. Still, officials took action, trimming Attucks's regular-season games in the fieldhouse to six. "I merely gave my personal advice to [Attucks principal] Dr. Lane," Phillips said, "and told him I thought it might be better if his schedule of games at Butler was not necessarily extended." Phillips emphasized to *Indianapolis Times* reporter Jimmie Angelopolous that he was not attempting "to dictate to anyone," but "just thought there would be less criticism if Attucks played a normal amount of games at Butler."[3]

But if Phillips was not "dictating," he was certainly suggesting with maximum force. Squeezing Attucks out of Butler was unprecedented. Before the controversy, any team had the option to acquire an open date at Butler Fieldhouse for 10 percent of gross receipts or three hundred dollars, whichever was higher. Now, without either Phillips or Butler president Maurice O. Ross explicitly stating a new policy, the rules had changed. It was similar to unwritten neighborhood codes in parts of the city; black applicants would be treated differently. "It's an unusual situation," remarked Dr. Lane. "Butler gave us the dates to play. Some of our dates were tentative because Butler has some extra things in the Fieldhouse this year."[4]

Of course, *Indianapolis Recorder* journalists could read between the lines of all the official statements and no-policy-change announcements. Attucks had always been "up the proverbial creek," and no matter what paddle the school tried to grab, some white official would attempt to snatch it back. So be it. If the Tigers were squeezed out of regular-season games at Butler, then that was that. But any Indianapolis school that made it to the state finals would play all its sectional, regional, semifinal, and final games at Butler. Regardless of the criticism or pressure, commented a *Recorder* editor, "it is possible for the Tigers to play 10 games in the big goal hall every year. And they can't be pressured out, or criticized out. They have to be shot out—every time."[5]

But how far in that magic ten-game series could Attucks realistically hope to go? Other state teams had won back-to-back championships, but did the Tigers have an honest chance? "Are We Gonna Repeat? . . . 'Does Ham Go With Eggs?'" bragged a full-page advertisement for the Tigers in the *Recorder*. But was that mere boosterism? The reality was that the 1954–55 team's two ball-hawking guards, Bill Scott and Bill Hampton, were gone,

Scott to Franklin College and Hampton to Indiana Central. The team's leading rebounders and inside players, Willie Merriweather and Sheddrick Mitchell, were also gone, Merriweather to Purdue and Mitchell to Butler. Four outstanding high school basketball players off to four different colleges. On a sociological level it was a near-miraculous achievement—sport living up to its loftiest ideal by giving four disadvantaged black youths a chance to receive a college education. But for Attucks's 1956 title aspirations it did not seem so hopeful.[6]

Only Oscar Robertson was left of the state championship five for Coach Ray Crowe to rebuild around, although no coach or reporter in Indianapolis could think of a better high school player than Oscar in Indiana—or in the United States for that matter—to serve as a linchpin. "Put Oscar with any group on any court in the country and when it came to dividing up for sides, Oscar was going to be the first one picked," remembered his assistant coach, Albert Spurlock. And Spurlock was not just remembering with twenty-twenty hindsight. Reporters said essentially the same thing even before the season started. "Watch Oscar Robertson this year, fans," observed one Jimmie Angelopolous. "He's going to be a unique high school basketball player." Two years had passed since Oscar made his varsity debut as a shy, gangly, fourteen-year-old sophomore. Now he was no longer an unknown. The "ivory hunters and goggle-eyed talent seekers" had placed him at the top of their preseason prep all-American team, and state sportswriters wrote that he was one of the best—if not the greatest—Hoosiers ever to play the game. He was sixteen and played as if he were going on twenty-five. Since the end of the previous season he had grown a little over an inch. When asked, he told reporters he was six feet, five inches. When questioned, he responded, "You want to measure me?"[7]

About some things, such as height, Robertson did not joke, and although he still did not bubble around reporters, he did give an impression of self-assurance, especially on the court. The other seniors on the team unquestioningly deferred to his judgment and instructions, while the underclassmen regarded him with a sense of awe. Oscar's friend Bill Swatts remembered that Robertson never aspired "to win any Mr. Nice Guy awards. On the court he was all business and single-minded in his pursuit of victory. When he was angry at someone, they knew it, though he did not always need to verbalize his feelings. Sometimes just a glance would do it." Edgar Searcy, one of the youngest members of the 1955–56 team, agreed that Oscar was a demanding leader but also an exceptionally fair one. "Oscar wanted you to think and take the game seriously. He would let you know if you messed up, but it wouldn't be in a put-down fashion. He would just tell you what to do the next time. Everyone knew he was the team leader, and he accepted that role. We knew that even if he didn't have a good shooting game, he would do the right thing."

Nor did such controversies as the Butler flap upset or sidetrack him. Oscar knew that his team had won the championship because it was the best team, not because it had played more games at Butler. "If they'd given us a decent gym in the first place we wouldn't have been in the position of having to play home games at Butler," he remembered. "Keeping us off the Fieldhouse floor was not going to save anybody." If anything, the controversy increased the team's desire to win another championship.[8]

Oscar was the leader and the star, but he was not the only talented player on the team. If Attucks had lost a group of exceptional players, another batch was on hand to take its place. From the nineteen students who tried out for the varsity team in the fall of 1955, Coach Crowe selected twelve players. "Bouncin'"

Billy Brown gave the Tigers rebounding and scoring strength in the frontcourt. Stan Patton was a forward who could shoot, play tight man-to-man defense, and keep the entire team loose with his offbeat observations and sense of humor. Albert Maxey's strength was effort. He was a guard who got in the face of shooters and was always eager to mix it up under the boards. Edgar Searcy was a skillful, fluid sophomore forward. Other players, including centers Odell Donel and John Gipson, forward James Enoch, and guards Henry Robertson, Sam Milton, and Lavern Benson, challenged the starters in practice and appeared ready to deliver when they were put in a game. "Looks pretty good," Crowe observed. "We have plenty of height and the boys all know how to use it."[9]

Team height, in fact, allowed Crowe to use Oscar as a guard. A 6'5" guard was rare enough in the collegiate or professional ranks; in high school it was practically blasphemy. Why take a player that tall away from the basket? Why assign him to defend a quicker guard? But Crowe knew what he was doing. He saw that Oscar could still take the ball to the hoop and help on the offensive and defensive boards. And he knew that there was not a quicker player than Robertson in the state. But most important, positioning Oscar at guard put the ball in his hands more and allowed him to control the game. "Nobody, I mean nobody, saw the whole court like Oscar," Searcy commented. "He seemed not only to know where every offensive and defensive player was on the court but also where they were going, what they would do next. He knew who to get the ball to, and when to just keep it himself." One of Oscar's opponents that year agreed, grumbling that Robertson probably also knew what the players on the bench were thinking.

If there were any lingering doubts about the team, they soon faded. The Tigers opened their season on a cold, snowy

Friday night with an away game against Fort Wayne Central. The previous year Central had won eighteen of twenty-one games and was one of the best teams in the state. Like Attucks, however, it had only one returning starter—and his name was not Oscar Robertson. Yet Central began the game with confidence, trailing by only eight points at the half. Jimmie Angelopolous of the *Indianapolis Times* noted that Attucks was not yet up to championship standards, and Central coach Herb Banet commented that the Tigers lacked the depth of the previous year's squad. In the second half, however, Attucks picked up the pace. Led by Robertson, who finished the game with thirty-one points, the Tigers hustled and shot over 50 percent, but even more startling was the speed of their play. Oscar constantly pushed the ball up the court, putting pressure on the defense and setting up his teammates for easy baskets. "I guess we did all right considering it was our first game," Coach Crowe commented after the 81-41 win.[10]

More difficult than the game was the ride home. A heavy snowfall and icy roads slowed the bus to a crawl, and it was nearly five in the morning when it arrived back in Indianapolis. A good night's sleep was out of the question; even a decent one was beyond hope. But thanks to Attucks's play-when-and-where-you-can schedule, it had a game in Indianapolis that night against its out-of-town rival Terre Haute Gerstmeyer. Sure enough, Attucks started slowly. The Tigers nursed a slim lead for most of the first quarter, then gave the 4,500 spectators crammed into the Tech gym a show, as they went on a 10-0 ninety-second burst. From that point on Attucks played for records, scoring ninety-eight points and shattering the eighty-six-point Tech floor record.[11]

"I'd hate to play them after they'd had a good night's sleep," commented a Terre Haute supporter, a thought shared by almost every reporter. Crispus Attucks, they emphasized, was *really good*. "Well, the whole state is buzzing now with the news that Attucks

IS as great this year as last year's squad," beamed *Indianapolis Recorder* reporter Jim Cummings. Like Attucks's other supporters he departed the east-side gym with the "Crazy Song" lingering in his ears and feeling "satisfied." Forget Butler, Cummings editorialized, the Tigers "can hit anywhere. Just put up two netted hoops on backboards and throw a basketball up in the middle of any old floor. They'll get the ball and put it through the hoops."[12]

After two games most reporters stopped comparing the Tigers to the previous year's team. In their first two outings they shot 50 percent and scored 179 points. Oscar himself scored 60 points, "more than a lot of high school players score in a season," according to Tech's athletic director. Several rival coaches worked their way into the crowded Tech gym while trying to remain "unseen"; they came away "awed" by Attucks's play and "puzzled" about how to stop the Tigers' fast-break offense. Oscar, in particular, attracted their interest. He excelled in every facet of the game, and as *Indianapolis Star* reporter Bob Collins suspected, he possessed "the ability to do a little unofficial coaching on the floor." It all added up as trouble for Attucks opponents.[13]

"I'll tell you this," remembered one white north-side basketball fan, "not everyone in Indianapolis was pleased with Attucks's success. Sure, it was nice that they won the title for the city, but they weren't the only school in the city, and some people wanted some of the success spread around." "Some people"— some white people—wanted to see Attucks beaten. It was not a desire that was openly voiced or written about in the local newspapers, but it was discussed over lunches at the Athletic Club and dinners in the downtown restaurants. It was part of the underground reaction to open competition, a belief that integration was good only up to a certain point. When open competition crossed over to African American domination, some white sensibilities were ruffled. Attucks was the first black team to fully, successfully achieve domination, and more than a few Hoosiers did not relish the fact.

But short of moving the hands on the race clock backward, there was nothing they could do about it. Ranked number one in the state, the Robertson-led Attucks team simply played on a higher level than the other teams. In its last game in November it played Sheridan, a team that was considered one of the finest in the state. Sheridan's plan was to slow down the game. But even though Attucks seemed flat, the Tigers still won by nineteen. Ten days later they traveled to South Bend Riley and put on an impressive exhibition, hitting their first six shots and winning the game 90-35.[14]

Some sportswriters predicted closer games once Attucks began to play the other city schools, but their prognostications were based more on generating interest and controversy than on actual evidence. After defeating Broad Ripple by thirteen points, Attucks prepared to meet Tech, its city rival. No longer, however, did the teams' styles contrast so starkly. The era of Charlie Maas's pattern offense had passed, or so *Recorder* reporter Jim Cummings believed. "This Tech team is a speedier one than the usually-cautious Mass [*sic*] aggregation," he commented. The reason, he implied, was that four of Tech's first six players were black. But at Tech old patterns persisted. Against Attucks, Tech employed a deliberate give-and-go offense and a box-and-one defense on Robertson, slowing down the game. It was a reasonably effective strategy. Attucks shot only 21 percent from the field and struggled throughout the contest. Midway through the third period the score was 27-27, and the momentum was on Tech's side. Then Bill Brown made two foul shots, Robertson stole a pass and drove three-quarters the length of the floor for a basket, and Tech's "charge" was over. In the fourth quarter Crowe switched his team into a zone and disrupted Maas's patterned offense. Although the Tigers won by seven points, they proved something more important to themselves: they could win even when they shot terribly and played against a defense designed to hold down Oscar.[15]

The night after Attucks defeated Tech at Butler, the Tigers played Ben Davis at Tech. Ben Davis liked to run, and it ran a lot that night—but it went nowhere. Attucks won by 43 points. Once again Robertson led all scorers with 33 points, but the points seemed secondary to his team play. "People talk about how much Oscar scored," recalled Ray Crowe, "but statistics never meant much to him. In most games I think he could have scored twice as many as he did. But he wanted first to win and second to keep everyone involved." But at the time, most of the reporters who covered the Attucks games dwelt on his numbers. Heading into the late-December city tournament, he had scored 191 points in seven games, a 27-point average. If he kept scoring at that pace, Bob Williams noted in the *Indianapolis Star,* he would score in the neighborhood of 600 points during the regular season and shatter the city record. "Unbelievable," "remarkable," "fantastic"— Williams and his fellow writers trafficked in superlatives when they wrote about Oscar.[16]

By its third year the city tournament had become the focal point of Indianapolis basketball, a post-Christmas present for thousands of basketball fans. Weeks before the game, city sportswriters began to discuss possible matchups, make predictions, and generate fan interest. Ferocious play was the norm, upsets common. But think as they might and speculate as they did, the journalists just could not see how any other city school could beat Attucks. Defending state champion, undefeated in its first seven games—Attucks was a "prohibitive favorite." A picture in the *Indianapolis Star* of five notable players in the city spoke volumes: in the center, framed by a single large star was a full-body drawing of Robertson. Surrounding him were the faces—bodiless faces—of the four other players, mere satellites orbiting planet Oscar.[17]

Sometimes, of course, even "prohibitive favorites" stumble. In its opening-round game against Washington on Wednesday night, Attucks played as if victory were some sort of divine right. Although Washington trailed most of the game it stayed within upset range. It held Oscar to three baskets in the first half and was down by only six points with six minutes remaining in the game. But then the Tigers broke the game open. As they had done all season, they demonstrated an ability to score quickly by playing tight defense, controlling both backboards, and scoring on fast breaks and tip-ins. In the last six minutes, Attucks scored twenty points and won the game 75-55.[18]

After beating Shortridge on Thursday afternoon in a poor-shooting semifinal contest, Attucks faced Tech Thursday night in the final game. Losing to Attucks had become something of a habit, one Tech wanted to break. Coach Charlie Maas realized the key to staying with Attucks was containing Robertson, and he used Freddie McCoy, shorter than Robertson but the state sprint champion, to dog Oscar all over the court. Throughout most of the game Tech successfully contained Attucks's fast break and smothered Oscar. Whenever Robertson drove for the basket he was sandwiched between two Tech players, with a shifting zone providing additional support. The strategy seemed to work. With only minutes left in the game Oscar had only eight points. When Tech tied the score 39-39 at the 3:10 mark in the final quarter, it looked as if it had a chance to win. But Robertson's confidence remained high. He wanted the ball, and he wanted the shot. He got the first and drove to the right, pulling up and shooting a twelve-foot baseline jumper. Every Tech player was within a step of him when he released the ball, but none could stop the shot that gave Attucks a two-point lead. The next time up the court Oscar tipped in a missed Attucks free throw, putting the Tigers up by five points and effectively icing the game. Fine play by Bill Brown and Oscar's brother Henry ensured the victory.[19]

Edgar Searcy recalled that the crucial, game-breaking jump shot was vintage Robertson: "Oscar didn't just play with natural ability; I think 50 percent of his game was pure mental. He never had an off-night because he was always thinking. He had a place on the court where he knew he could make seven or eight out of ten jump shots. His spot was down low on the right side. When we needed the bucket Oscar took McCoy to his spot and made the shot. That's skill, but it's also thinking. Most seventeen-year-old kids never think like that."

The year ended with Attucks fans looking both to the past and future. Behind them was a state championship, the top sports story in the *Indianapolis Star*'s year-end review and the most important event of the decade along Indiana Avenue. Ahead was the possibility of another championship. Lafayette Jefferson was ranked second in the state, but after watching Jeff in its holiday tournament Jim Cummings of the *Indianapolis Recorder* concluded that although "Lafayette has everything—height, experience, depth, desire and coaching . . . they still don't look like Tiger eaters."[20]

Success on the basketball court, however, had not solved many of black Indianapolis's or black America's most pressing problems. Bob Collins of the *Indianapolis Star* wrote that Crowe and his team had "pounded down the wall." But segregation was still the order of the day. Even as the Tigers were playing their December games, the *Recorder* was covering a controversy in Louisiana where some Sugar Bowl officials insisted that the University of Pittsburgh not use its single black player and not sell its block of tickets on an integrated basis. Georgia Tech was scheduled to play Pittsburgh, and Georgia governor Marvin Griffin weighed in on the controversy with the opinion that Tech should not play in the game if Pittsburgh planned on using a black athlete.[21]

Such stories recorded the very lack of racial progress that some people touted sports as promoting. The irony was not lost on black journalists, especially those in Indianapolis. What difference had Attucks made in Indiana and America? Had athletic excellence and sterling sportsmanship advanced the cause of their race? These questions remained open. *Recorder* editorialist Andrew W. Ramsey rejoiced over Attucks's championship and applauded the movement, albeit glacial, toward the desegregation of Indianapolis schools. But Attucks remained "totally pupiled" by blacks, and little integration had occurred in white neighborhoods. The police department continued to be segregated, as did the fire department, and it was uncertain whether mayor-elect Philip Bayt would include blacks on his policy-making boards. How long would blacks have to wait for real change? How many years would have to drag by before the promise of the *Brown* decision was fully realized?[22]

But the country was stirring, more so than Ramsey knew. As Ramsey wrote his editorial, blacks in Montgomery, Alabama, planned a front. On December 1, 1955, Rosa Parks, a black seamstress and local secretary for the NAACP, had left her job at a department store for her usual bus ride home. The bus was crowded and she had sat in the front row of the "colored" section. Soon all the seats were taken, filled by fourteen whites in the front of the bus and twenty-two blacks in the back. When another white man boarded, the driver, exercising his Jim Crow right, told the first row of blacks seated in "no-man's-land" to get up and stand in the back. A weary Parks simply refused, even when the driver told her she would be arrested if she did not vacate her seat. She told the driver that he could do what he pleased, but she was not moving. In short order she was arrested, booked, fingerprinted, and locked in a jail. And unknown to her, unknown to anybody on that particular day, she and her people crossed a symbolic Rubicon. Years later black activist Eldridge Cleaver observed that on that cold December day "somewhere in the universe a gear in the machinery shifted."[23]

Parks's arrest led to a chain of events that culminated with the emergence of Martin Luther King Jr. as the leader of the Montgomery Bus Boycott. The bus boycott would last 381 days— 381 days of organized carpooling, determined walking, and peaceful protests, 381 days that demonstrated the discipline, resolve, faith, and economic power of Montgomery's black community. "There comes a time," King said on the first night of the boycott, "when people get tired . . . tired of being segregated and humiliated, tired of being kicked about by the brutal feet of oppression. . . . For many years we have shown amazing patience. . . . But we've come here tonight to be saved from that patience that makes us patient with anything less than freedom and justice."[24]

Although the players might not have realized it, the Attucks team of Oscar Robertson's junior year was part of King's impatience with patience. So too was the 1955–56 team. Its goal was to demonstrate, completely and beyond a shred of doubt, that it was the finest high school basketball team in the state of Indiana. The fact that the team was all black spoke for itself. Nobody, not the players and their fans or their opponents and their supporters, missed the point that race was important, that it dictated the subtext for everything Attucks did on the court. Each victory, the product of teamwork and individual excellence, was like a day in Montgomery: proof positive that a change was taking place along the color line.

The Tigers began 1956 as they had ended 1955—by winning. In their eleventh game of the season they defeated South Bend Adams by thirty-seven points. The game was something of a lovefest, more a cleanly played exhibition than a competitive game. Most of the Attucks players scored, everyone saw action, and the South Bend players seemed to enjoy just being on the same court with the fabled Tigers. More than anything else it was a game to get the Tigers back into a routine after the holiday. Ahead on their schedule was Michigan City, the bruising squad from the Region. The year before, the game had featured some of the roughest and dirtiest play of the year, and Jim Cummings expected more of the same in 1956.[25]

Michigan City worried Coach Crowe. The game the year before occurred about the time that Attucks descended into a minor slump. "Last year at this time we were going stale," he told sportswriter Bob Collins on the afternoon before the game. "We had a big winning streak then, too, and the pressure was getting hard to take. It was so bad it was almost a relief when we finally lost one." This season, however, Crowe was in no mood for the "relief" that a loss might deliver. He liked the streak, liked the steady diet of victories, and loathed the idea of a loss, a slump, or a stale team. The game against Michigan City, a tough squad with eight wins and four losses on the season, promised to tell Crowe something about his own team. But he had an odd feeling. These players did not need a loss to relieve pressure or gain motivation. They were driven by the desire for greatness. "They want to do better than the state championship team," he said. "The only way they can is win them all." And Crowe, though he almost feared to articulate it, believed that a perfect season was a distinct possibility. "I don't know why but I just feel we are going to hit our peak pretty soon," he told reporters. "Sometimes you can sense things like that. They seem to want to play this one. So we should know a little more after tonight's game."[26]

The game told him something, besides the fact that he was "batting—roughly—1,000 in the intuition league," as Collins put it. The result screamed out that Attucks was very, very good, far better than he or anyone else had even suspected. The Tigers did not just defeat Michigan City, they humiliated the northern school. Attucks connected on its first seven shots, scored thirty-nine points in the first quarter, and sixty-one in the first half. The second half was more of the same. Attucks scored another thirty-five points in the third quarter and won the game 123-53. Oscar accounted for forty-five points—breaking Hallie Bryant's single-game city-county record—but that still left seventy-eight points for his teammates to divide among themselves. Jim Cummings was not ready to say that he had seen the best Attucks team, but he did admit "on that particular day [it] was the greatest team ever to wear the Attucks uniform." An Associated Press reporter agreed, noting that "Attucks could slide considerably from its Saturday night peak and still have an excellent chance to repeat as IHSAA king."[27]

The Michigan City game was the basketball equivalent of an atomic explosion. Its fallout scattered across the state, increasing both interest in and fear of Attucks. Now more people than ever wanted to watch the "celebrated Tigers." For Attucks's next game, a Tuesday-night contest against Shortridge, some eight thousand spectators crowded into Butler Fieldhouse. The contest pitted the city's two highest scorers, Robertson and Herschell Turner, against each other, but it was hardly a two-man show. Although Oscar led all scorers with twenty-two points, he received solid support from his brother Henry, who started the game, Stanford Patton, and underclassmen Edgar Searcy and Albert Maxey. Attucks won the game by ten points, but it was not the score or anyone's play in particular that attracted the most attention.[28]

Officiating had once again become an issue. The *Recorder* sportswriters had complained for years that white officials not only consistently called more fouls on Attucks players than on their opponents, but that the close, crucial calls at the end of the game normally went against the Tigers. Although the definition of a crucial foul had become blurred—how crucial could any foul be in a forty- or fifty-point victory?—biased officials, at least in theory, presented several problems. First, they altered Crowe's lineup. In the Shortridge game, for example, fouls forced both Bill Brown and Stanford Patton to spend significant time on the bench and tested the quality of the Tigers' reserves. Second, they awarded more free throws to Attucks's opponents. Attucks outscored Shortridge 54-26 from the field, but Shortridge stayed in the game from the free-throw line, making thirty of forty-one in the game and twenty-two of twenty-five in the second half. In the end, because the officials called more than twice as many fouls on Attucks, Shortridge managed to keep the game close.

0It was not just the fouls officials called on Attucks that concerned Crowe and Indianapolis sportswriters; it was the ones that they did not call on the Tigers' opponents. Some journalists suspected that officials had decided to treat Robertson like a race-horse and handicap him. When Oscar drove for the hoop, opponents hand-checked him, slapped at his hands, and bodied him with impunity. "Apparently," Bob Collins observed, "it's open season on Oscar Robertson." He had noticed that "sometimes officials—intentionally or otherwise—allow a boy who is a little better or bigger than his opponents [to] take a bit more of a shoving around before they blow that whistle," and it seemed to him that "a foul against Oscar is as much a foul as it is against anyone else." At least Collins could not discover any Oscar "exemptions" in the rule book.[29]

Indianapolis Star columnist Jep Cadou Jr. agreed that officials were singling out Robertson for special—or especially bad—treatment. The referees seemed blind when Oscar was hacked and pushed, but they watched his defense with a jeweler's eye. "In a way, Oscar might prove to be the victim of his own brilliance," said Cadou. "If it seems that officials are calling fouls awfully close on him, it is likely to be because the eyes of the boys in the striped shirts are on him most of the time. Someone else may get away with murder while Oscar is being penalized." The question was, as Cadou saw it, "How good a basketball team would Crispus Attucks be without Oscar Robertson?" With him, no doubt about it, the Tigers were the finest in the state. Without him their "bubble might burst in a hurry."[30]

Attucks's fourteenth game of the season was a case in point. In an intense contest against city rival Washington, Attucks started strong, building a lead in the first quarter, improving on it in the second, and enjoying one of its patented spurts in the third. With five and a half minutes remaining in the period the Tigers led by twenty-one points. Crowe put in a few reserves, and Washington closed the gap to fourteen points, but there seemed no legitimate cause for concern. With twenty-seven seconds left in the third quarter Oscar picked up his fourth foul. "Then, Boom!" wrote Jim Cummings. "A package of fissionable material . . . exploded and the Tigers began slipping and sliding and Tiger fans began praying."[31]

While Crowe sat stone-faced, upset by the officiating, Washington scored nine straight points in less than three minutes. "During that brief span, Attucks didn't look like the same ball club," noted Cadou. Crowe took a risk and sent Oscar back into the game, and Robertson played cautiously on defense while he stabilized the offense. With Oscar back in the game Attucks settled down, winning by five points. But what would have happened if Robertson had picked up his fifth foul? Or if Crowe had kept him on the bench a minute or two longer? After the Shortridge game Jimmie Angelopolous had confidently asserted that Attucks would win another state championship and that Robertson was "one of the greatest players Indiana has ever seen." Few could doubt his assessment of Oscar, or even Attucks's chances to repeat with Robertson, but if the Tiger star fouled out of a game, or if he sprained an ankle, then the gap between Attucks and the field narrowed.[32]

The Washington game was more of a blip than a trend. The sum of the Tigers was more than the product of one player. Even without Oscar, Attucks was a superb team. Brown was the best rebounder in the city, Patton was remarkably steady, and four or five other players competed for the other two positions. Albert Maxey, Henry Robertson, Edgar Searcy, Sam Milton, and John Gipson all contributed to Attucks's success. "With Oscar, Patton, and Brown as a nucleus," Searcy recalled, "it didn't really matter who the other two players were. To be honest, you might be able to trim it down to Oscar and one of the other two." The possibility that they would all have off-games on the same night was slim. In the games following the Washington scare, Attucks was not challenged. The Tigers defeated Howe by thirty-one points and Gary's Lew Wallace by fifty-four; then they faced Connersville, the team that had beaten them by one point the year before.[33]

Once again Connersville had a strong team, and more than nine thousand spectators paid to see if the "Tiger slayers" could do it again. But without freak weather conditions and icy floors, Connersville was no match for Attucks. From the start of the contest until the game was long out of reach, Oscar controlled the action, scoring when he wanted to and setting up his teammates for good shots. He tallied twenty-one points; it could have been more. "He could hit considerablely [*sic*] more points than he does," commented a *Recorder* writer. "But first he is a team man." However, the reporter added, "one of these nights, after victory is assured, Crowe might turn Oscar loose and say 'go get those 49 points.'"[34]

Exactly how many points Robertson could score if the urge moved him generated fine speculative discussions, especially as Attucks got ready to play some of the weaker teams on its schedule. He had scored forty-five, so that offered a starting point for debates, but whether he could put up fifty or fifty-five separated the realists from those with their heads in the clouds. The debate gained seriousness when Washington's Jerry Lawlis broke Oscar's city record, scoring forty-eight in an overtime game against Speedway. Of course, *Indianapolis Star* sportswriter Bob Williams speculated, Crowe would not allow Oscar to go for the record at the expense of a "clean slate," but "it stands to reason the No. 1 team in the state will try to get the record back for Oscar." After the Connersville victory, Robertson had four regular-season games left to try for the record. In a four-day stretch Attucks would play three city schools—Cathedral, Manual, and Sacred Heart—then finish its regular season a week later against Frankfort. Four games, four virtually guaranteed victories—certainly Coach Crowe would allow Oscar to cut loose in one of them.[35]

Attucks played sluggishly in the first half of its game against Cathedral, making only eight of its thirty-one shots. The Tigers played better in the second half, winning 65-44, and Oscar scored 26 points, breaking his own city record of 449 single-season points. The Manual game followed the same pattern. Attucks won by 24 points but scored only 64. Actually, neither game was conducive to scoring records. Both were played on

Butler's college-length court, giving Cathedral and Manual more space to slow down the game and avoid traps.[36]

The Sacred Heart game was scheduled for Tech's gym, a smaller, more scoring-friendly court. Crowe wanted to give Oscar a chance at the record, but he faced a cruel dilemma. He liked Sacred Heart, its coach, and its players. The Catholic school had played Attucks back when other city schools would not schedule games against the Tigers. Together the schools had faced prejudice, one based on race, the other on religion; together they had battled to get into the IHSAA, coming into the organization the same year. Crowe had no desire to embarrass Sacred Heart, but Oscar, who had never gone into a game thinking about his own statistics, deserved the shot. Crowe discussed the problem with Oscar's teammates. What did they think? Oscar was their friend, their leader, a role model to many of them, and besides, he was the most gifted, unselfish basketball player they could imagine. It was simple justice   only fitting—that he hold the record. "It was Mr. Crowe's decision," remembered Edgar Searcy, "but we supported it; we thought he deserved it. Oscar didn't have any input."

From the moment the game began it was clear that no Attucks player was going to prevent Oscar from recapturing the record. When he passed the ball to Brown or Patton or any other teammate, they simply passed it back and told him to shoot. They were not interested in a Robertson assist. So he shot and he scored and he shot and he scored, and he just kept repeating the action. "He hit from under, from slightly out, from out and from 'way out," noted the *Recorder* reporter. "He hit the layups, the hooks, the shovels, the jumps, and the set shots. He was superb." He scored twenty of his team's twenty-three points in the first period; his brother Henry scored the other three.[37]

When the Spartans of Sacred Heart saw that the Attucks players would give up an uncontested layup to pass off to Oscar, they began to triple-team him. Sometimes all the Spartans on the floor surrounded him. But it did not really matter. His teammates continued their informal shooting boycott—they took only eleven shots—and Oscar kept scoring. He scored ten more points in the second quarter and ten in the third. In the fourth quarter, in an effort to get Sacred Heart to shoot faster, Attucks "virtually quit" playing defense, and Oscar added twenty-two more to his total. On the night, he tallied sixty-two points on twenty-three of sixty from the field and sixteen of twenty-two from the foul line.[38]

"Call him Oscar anything—that is anything on the list of adjectives that doesn't go below 'magnificent,'" wrote the *Recorder* sportswriter, expressing the attitude of the spectators and journalists at the game. Attucks fans cheered and chanted, shook their heads in appreciation, and laughed with delight, enjoying the pure joy of watching one of their own explore uncharted ground. Robertson's teammates were also trapped in the moment. They passed the ball to Oscar as if they were giving him a Christmas present that they planned to enjoy as much as he. From the bench and sometimes even from the court they cheered every shot Oscar took, trying, it seemed, through some collective psychic will to guide the ball through the hoop. Only Oscar seemed slightly outside the shared experience, as if he were slightly embarrassed by all the attention. For him basketball had always been the ultimate team game, and turning it into an individual exhibition seemed to offend his sense of how the game should be played.[39]

It would have been a fitting end to an exemplary regular season—but Attucks still had to play Frankfort, a fine team with an even better basketball tradition. Attucks began the game against Frankfort as it had ended the Sacred Heart contest—playing virtually no defense. The only difference was that Oscar was not scoring on offense. Time and time again a Frankfort guard drove past his defender, forced a switch, then passed off for an uncontested shot. Toward the end of the first quarter the Hot Dogs led 15-6, and the normally impassive Crowe registered mild concern, which for him meant that he leaned back, looked up, took a deep breath, and slowly exhaled.

Crowe called time-out to make a tactical change. He switched to a zone defense, a move that paid immediate dividends. Back-to-back steals and layups by Stanford Patton closed the gap to 15-10 at the end of the quarter. By the half, Attucks was up by four, a lead it stretched to eleven at the end of the third quarter. Frankfort never made another run, Crowe substituted liberally, and Attucks won 52-42, finishing its regular season 21-0. It was the first time an Indianapolis school had gone through a regular season undefeated, and it raised Attucks's unbeaten streak to thirty five, three short of the state record. If the Tigers won the four games necessary to gain their fourth-straight sectional crown, they would break the record. For a segregated school without a home court, Crispus Attucks High School had done well.[40]

Chapter Seven

ONE YEAR BETTER THAN THE BEST EVER

The 1955–56 Crispus Attucks Tigers had performed well, but not well enough to satisfy their faithful, who alternately predicted, demanded, and expected, hoped and prayed for, another state title. If a person wanted to make a wager—and many people did—on the outcome of the state tournament, there were 742 teams from which to choose. Seven hundred and forty-two teams—but only one had short odds. Anybody with any basketball sense picked Attucks to repeat. Bob Collins picked Attucks, though that was hardly news; he frequently predicted the Tigers would take it all. Jep Cadou Jr. picked Southport, again unsurprisingly; he had always seemed supremely confident that Attucks, no matter what its record, would fall short in a big game. Across the state, other sportswriters and sportscasters made their calls. The Associated Press asked thirty-five of them to sound off. Almost unanimously they voted Attucks as the state's outstanding team, but only fifteen thought the Tigers would repeat as state champions. Lafayette, Seymour, and Kokomo received four votes each, with the rest of the votes scattered. Of the thirty-five invited prognosticators, not one came from the staff of the *Indianapolis Recorder* or any of the state's other black newspapers.[1]

The *Recorder,* like Attucks players and officials, played it close to the vest. The paper was full of the usual clichés—"nobody is 'booked to win,'" "nothing is certain," "not one [team] rolls over dead." But the clichés seemed to mask feelings of conviction and utter confidence. Attucks had a good draw, a better team, and the best player in the state. Perhaps nobody would roll over and play dead, but somebody, presumably still alive, would have to cover Oscar Robertson.[2]

For west-side readers of the *Indianapolis Recorder,* the "B" words—basketball and boycott—dominated the news and became part of a fabric of racial pride. On March 3, 1956, the *Recorder*'s headline announced "One-Hour Work Stoppage to Spotlight Bus Boycott," and the accompanying story detailed plans for a nationwide strike to demonstrate solidarity with ninety Montgomery blacks arrested for their part in the boycott. The strike, scheduled between 2 P.M. and 3 P.M. on March 28, a "national deliverance day of prayer," would be a "national Mohandas Gandhi–type movement," suggested New York congressman Adam Clayton Powell Jr. Below the headline and beside the story, however, was a feature detailing the exploits of the Crispus Attucks Tigers. The point was impossible to overlook; the main stories in Montgomery and Indianapolis were part of the same long, progressive struggle for justice and advancement. There may have been some corner of Indiana where basketball was just basketball, but that corner was not the west side of Indianapolis. There basketball was sacred, connecting to notions of racial progress, racial pride, and racial accomplishments. It was the visible, outward expression of what was and what might be.[3]

In that context, victory and defeat were loaded with additional layers of meaning, a burden that Attucks players had always knowingly shouldered. Defeat entailed not just personal failure, not just team failure, but letting down one's community and race. It was an intense pressure, one that never really went away. An Attucks player wearing a letter sweater received special treatment along Indiana Avenue and in its restaurants; an honored guest, he received smiles and free dinners without asking. The payback came on game day. No one had to say, "Don't lose. Make us proud." That went with the turf. The player knew—his teammates knew—that an Attucks loss would make another team's season and quietly please most of the state. The only answer: "We won't lose."

That was the attitude of Ray Crowe and his team as they prepared for sectional play. In past years Attucks supporters had complained that officials had stacked the Indianapolis sectional against the Tigers. That protest was not heard in 1956. In the top half of the draw, Shortridge and Tech, two of Attucks's traditional foes, had to play each other in the first round. In contrast, Attucks was tucked in the bottom half of the draw with weaker schools such as Beech Grove, Wood, the Indiana Deaf School, and Cathedral. This meant that Attucks would be fresh for the biggest games, not tired from having to play all the best teams.[4]

Attucks opened the sectional against Beech Grove. The experts said it would be no contest. They were right. The Tigers jumped to a 15-2 lead, finished the half leading 40-8, and coasted to a 91-30 victory. The next two contests proved a bit more testing, however. During the regular season Howe had played a slowed-down game and lost by thirty-one points. This time it attempted to run with Attucks and lost by only fourteen points. In the Saturday-afternoon semifinal game Attucks played Cathedral's Fighting Irish, which had upset Manual the night before. The Irish played with confidence, intelligence, and grit; they committed only six turnovers, scrapped for every loose ball, and kept the game close. They led by one at the quarter, trailed by two at the half, and were down by only three at the conclusion of the third period. Oscar made the difference in the fourth quarter. Playing with four fouls, he made two straight shots to stretch the Attucks lead to seven and effectively seal the game. Crowe viewed the eight-point victory as a wake-up call. The easy games were over; now his team had to perform.[5]

Shortridge survived the battles in the upper bracket for the right to play Attucks in the evening finals. Led by Herschell Turner, one of the most gifted athletes in the state, Shortridge's players "believed" they could win. Attucks, they reasoned, was not up to full strength. Stanford Patton had injured his foot in the Howe game, sat out the Cathedral contest, and looked doubtful for the evening finals. Throughout the season Patton had relieved some of the offensive pressure from Oscar. Though not tall, he was skilled at flashing to the high post, taking a pass from Oscar, then scoring on a turnaround jumper. "The shot never got blocked," Edgar Scarcy recalled. "I once asked Patton how he did it. He said, 'Easy. Oscar passes the ball, and I fake a return pass. Then everybody rushes toward Oscar, and I shoot.'" But with Patton injured and Oscar a thoroughly known commodity, there seemed little chance that the eyes and hands of the Shortridge players would ever leave the Attucks star.

From the opening tip Shortridge played confidently. Before the game was two minutes old, the Blue Devils led 6-0, and they increased the lead to 10-2, forcing Coach Crowe to call time-out to calm his players. He told them they were the better team, but they needed to play like it, and he sent a badly limping Patton into the game. When the first quarter ended two and a half minutes later, the game was tied 12-12. The second quarter was like the first—a series of spurts. In the first minute Attucks took the lead and increased it to 18-12. Then Turner led his team back. In the most exciting play of the tournament, the teams exchanged jump shots and drives and free throws. When the horn ended the half, the Tigers led by one point.[6]

The two teams clawed at each other throughout the second half. Bill Brown was having an off-night, and Patton was doing as well as he could on a gimpy foot, but other players had to perform. Searcy played well, and reserve Lavern Benson, a 5'5" guard who had not seen much action during the regular season, was all over the court, hustling, deflecting passes, and making a few important baskets. But as it had so often in the past, the game came down to Oscar Robertson. Could the "Great One," as the *Recorder* sportswriter called him, deliver when the Tigers needed him most?

Shortridge players did their best to stop Oscar. They defended him with a box-and-one, constantly double- and triple-teaming him, but throughout the second half when Attucks needed a basket, Oscar responded. He also played tough defense. In the first half Crowe had employed a zone defense, and Turner had scored twelve points; in the second Crowe shifted to man-to-man with Robertson on Turner, and the Shortridge leader scored only one more field goal. Paced by Oscar's twenty-four points and stout defending, Attucks won 53-48. "That big guy was the difference," Shortridge coach Cleon Reynolds told reporters after the game. "When the pressure was on that Oscar Robertson was right there."[7]

When the game ended, the ball, appropriately enough, was in Oscar's hands at the north end of the Butler court. He "let loose a tremendous heave," throwing the ball into the south-end stands. It was worth a small celebration. After the game, as the Shortridge players slumped off the court, wiping away tears with the back of their hands, and as the Shortridge cheerleaders cried openly, Attucks fans rushed the court. It was a wild, happy scene. Players hugged, then looked for Shortridge players to congratulate. Fans hugged, then looked for other fans to hug. Photographers tried to get the players to pose; a few near a basket obliged by leaping up, grabbing the rim, swinging on it, and climbing on the backboard, while Ray Crowe and Athletic Director Lon Watford looked on with concern. Radio and television commentators and newspaper reporters scrambled about looking for players to interview. "I'm really living," Lavern Benson shouted. Flashbulbs exploded, camera shutters clicked, announcers talked, and above it all was the rock 'n' roll sound of "Tweedle Dee."[8]

In the corridor leading to the locker rooms Reynolds waited for Crowe. He shook Crowe's hand and said, "Now go all the way." Crowe thanked him, then turned his attention to his players. Patton was still limping. Benson's plate had been knocked out in the Howe game, and he was suffering from a gashed gum. But Oscar was fine. That was something to celebrate.[9]

The victory gave Crispus Attucks supporters a few extra treats to appreciate. Several city and state records fell. It was their fourth-straight sectional victory; no city school had ever accomplished that feat. Before Attucks's run none had ever won more than two consecutively, and now the Tigers had captured five of the last six. In addition, the win extended Attucks's winning streak to thirty-nine, breaking a state record that had lasted thirty-four years. "That's 39 straight, guys, isn't it?" Oscar asked after the game, and a few of his teammates repeated, "39, 39, 39." If the all-black team needed anything else to set it apart, the records did it.[10]

But the celebrations were not drawn out. Ray Crowe knew, Oscar Robertson knew, and the other Attucks players knew that if they lost their next game or if they failed to win the state title, then the four sectionals in a row, the thirty-nine straight victories, would lose something of their meaning. So after a few giddy moments they settled down, dressed quietly, and started to think about the next hurdle. The regional tournament was a week away.

In theory, games became progressively tougher the further a team advanced in the state tournament. Reality, however, was different. Four games in the Indianapolis sectional, usually three difficult ones, often proved more taxing than the regional tournament. This was the case in 1956. In the afternoon game of the Indianapolis regional Attucks drew Anderson, the fifth-ranked team in the state. Anderson was experienced and fast, but also woefully short—its tallest player stood less than six feet, one inch. Even its experience was something of a liability. All of its starters had played against Attucks in the previous year's regional and had been soundly whipped 76-51.[11]

Although sportswriters spent the week detailing the serious inequities between the teams, their articles did not keep fans away. Nearly fourteen thousand spectators filled Butler Fieldhouse to see if Anderson could upset the local Goliath. Attucks swiftly answered that question. Anderson won the tip, and Attucks fell back in a zone that was so tight it seemed like a man-to-man defense. Twenty-three seconds into the game Anderson coach Ick Osborne called time-out to instruct his players to go into their zone offense, a tactic that made no difference. Anderson players tried to throw passes over the zone; they attempted to overload one side and to probe for an opening with short passes; they experimented with shooting over it and driving through it. Nothing worked against what a *Recorder* sportswriter called "the best zone defense this state has seen in a long, long time." Attucks, finding little trouble scoring and completely controlling both boards, quickly built a comfortable lead and kept it. Paced by Robertson's twenty points—all scored in the first three quarters—Attucks won 61-48. Had Crowe not substituted freely in the last quarter, the outcome would have been much worse.[12]

On paper Anderson had looked like Attucks's most difficult challenge in the regional tournament, and that's the way it turned out to be. The evening contest against Hancock Central was a mismatch of epic proportions. Attucks led 24-3 at the end of the first quarter and 58-17 at the half, winning the game 99-43. If it had been a boxing match the referee would have stopped it early in the first quarter to prevent anyone from getting hurt, a humane consideration that would have suited the Attucks faithful just fine. Because with just over five minutes remaining in the second quarter an Attucks player drove for the basket, soared high above the rest of the players, and laid the ball in the hoop, putting his team ahead 38-8. As he came down, a Hancock Central player slid under him, taking out his legs and throwing him headfirst toward the floor. The Attucks player instinctively reached out in a futile attempt to break his fall. As he struggled to his feet he had a pained look on his face. He held his right wrist, and his right hand "dangled limply."[13]

For a moment it seemed that every Attucks player and fan held one large collective breath. "Oh Please God, Not Oscar," cried a green-and-gold-clad Attucks supporter. "When Oscar hit the floor," one reporter later wrote, "Ray Crowe was out there so fast someone threw him a pass." It was clear from the way he slumped to the bench and from the concerned look on Crowe's face that Robertson was hurt, perhaps badly. "I thought it was something serious," Crowe remembered. "Maybe broken. Maybe ligaments. I feared the worst."[14]

Oscar was done for the evening—but how much longer no one knew. Attucks trainer Sam Johnson put the worst fears to rest. The immediate cause of the player's pain was a dislocated thumb, and the trainer popped it back into place. At halftime Butler trainer Jim Morris examined Oscar's hand through a fluoroscope and found no evidence of a broken bone. After the game

Robertson was taken to Saint Vincent Hospital, where a technician X-rayed his hand. The next morning a doctor pronounced Oscar's hand fine—nothing broken, no bone chips, no ligament damage.[15]

But the week passed in a cloud of speculation. The news of the week—the racial brouhaha at the University of Alabama, the Supreme Court affirming the *Brown* decision, France granting Morocco independence—seemed secondary in Indianapolis. The central question was: would Oscar be ready? Photographs of his injured hand and stories of his trips to Butler for treatment filled newspaper space. Everybody assumed he would suit up and play. But would he be effective? Would his shooting hand flap with its usual precision?

Actually, the hand healed quickly. Oscar practiced and competed, hit shots and drove hard. He showed no signs of worry and did not seem hampered by his injury. Stanford Patton had also recovered from his ankle problem. Bill Brown had emerged from a slump, sophomore Edgar Searcy was playing with more confidence, and to most observers Attucks appeared to be peaking at just the right time. The team certainly exuded a quiet confidence, possessing an "almost utter contempt for pressure," *Indianapolis Star* reporter Jep Cadou Jr. noted later. "The Tigers are many things. They are remarkable shooters, tireless rebounders, speedy runners, fancy dribblers, shifty fakers, ballhawking guards. But above all they are the epitome of the CCC—cool, calm and collected." And they were one other thing, the one thing that white reporters never mentioned—intelligent players. They understood the game, and their calmness came from a knowledge that they played it better than any other high school team.[16]

Connersville coach Ken Gunning matched Attucks's confidence, though his manner was not so quiet. His team had drawn Attucks in the afternoon semifinal game, and he said that he planned on coaching his players in the evening championship. "Sure we think we can whip Attucks," he said. Connersville had done it a year ago, and the team could do it again. The press liked Gunning, mostly because he provided good copy. Like many coaches he was compulsively superstitious; on his way into Rushville for the regionals he had convinced the bus driver to take a long way into town rather than cross a particularly "unlucky" iron bridge. He had also told reporters and his team that if Connersville won the regional tournament, he would run all the way home. Connersville did win, and though he did not make the entire cross-county jog, he did stop the bus outside the city limits and run into town, much to the delight of photographers.[17]

A man who devotes much of his energy thinking about iron bridges and traveling routes has little time left for things as small as top-ranked opponents. Sure, Attucks was good, Gunning confessed, but he was of the mind that coaches worried too much about how to stop the Tigers. He felt other teams worried so much about stopping Attucks's offense that "they never do much offensively" themselves. Gunning was not about to make the same mistake. He realized that Robertson was the "best player" but did not plan to do anything out of the ordinary to contain him. "We won't concentrate on Oscar. He'll get his 20 or 30 points anyway." Besides, Robertson's 24.3-points-a-game average paled next to the question of routes into Indianapolis.[18]

Judging from his team's performance at Butler Fieldhouse on March 10, Gunning decided on the wrong route into town. Attucks controlled every phase of the game, especially scoring and rebounding. Bill Brown and Oscar alone grabbed more rebounds than the entire Connersville team, and Attucks built an early lead and never lost it, coasting to a 67-49 victory and setting up an evening final against Scottsburg.

Like Attucks, the Scottsburg Warriors were playing their best basketball in the tournament. In the competitive Columbus regional they had defeated Southport, a team some experts had picked to win the state title, and then knocked out traditional powerhouse Muncie Central in the afternoon semifinal game. They had lost only two games during the regular season, and they had become media darlings. No sooner had they defeated Southport than sportswriters began comparing them to Milan, the 1954 state champion. Back then Milan had defeated Crispus Attucks on its way to the title, and several reporters suggested— none predicted—that this Milan clone could do the same.

But when Milan defeated Attucks, Oscar Robertson was still a sophomore, and several of his teammates were injured. Now Oscar was an experienced, confident senior, and his teammates were healthy. Once the game started it was obvious that Scottsburg was overmatched. Sensing as much, the Scottsburg players attempted to play at Attucks's faster pace and fell behind 12-4. Eventually Scottsburg settled down and fought hard, but it made little difference. Led by Oscar, Attucks played in complete control. It did not have a turnover in the first half and capitalized on Scottsburg's mistakes. Throughout the second half Attucks maintained its lead and won the contest 67-42. It seemed so routine. As in so many of its tournament games, Attucks's plan seemed to be to get an early ten-point lead, match its opponent bucket-for-bucket for a stretch, "then really roll." It was an efficiency that wore down the opponents and quieted even Attucks's own fans. There seemed to be a real possibility that the 1956 state tournament would be transformed into a Crispus Attucks exhibition.[19]

During the following week Crispus Attucks in particular and the black community in Indianapolis in general prepared for another state championship. Once again the *Indianapolis Recorder* blossomed with well-wishes. Loan companies, restaurants, beauty salons, construction companies, pharmacies, cleaners, liquor stores—businesses of every description and size bought space. So did churches, fraternal organizations, and private individuals. "Go Tigers, Go Our Tigers" was the heart of their messages.

Expecting victory, black-community leaders wanted to avoid another postgame embarrassment. The previous year they had not planned a downtown celebration and after a humiliatingly brief stop at Monument Circle had been escorted back to their own district. But a committee made up of the mayor, police chief, fire chief, superintendent of schools, and representatives of the park board and chamber of commerce decided that there would be no significant change. Dr. Russell Lane announced that if Attucks won—or even if it was runner-up—the celebrations would commence immediately with a motor parade. It would start in the Butler Fieldhouse parking lot, proceed east on Forty-ninth Street and south on Meridian, and stop at the Circle. Once again, the Circle celebrations would be limited—five minutes for yells and songs; no speeches. Then back into the cars and buses and fire trucks to west Indianapolis—to familiar North-western Park—for a bonfire and more extended celebrations.[20]

The plan disappointed many of Attucks's supporters, but not enough for them to lose sight of the importance of the state finals. "We wanted to win," Ray Crowe remembered. "That was something we could control. The rest was out of our hands. Unimportant. People would only remember who won." With that in mind, he prepared his team to play Terre Haute Gerstmeyer and the winner of the Lafayette Jefferson–Elkhart tilt.

Seldom in the history of Indiana basketball had Hoosiers regarded the state tournament as such an afterthought. The Crispus Attucks Tigers had won forty-three straight games, most by embarrassingly lopsided scores. They had rolled through sectional, regional, and semifinal play, in the process making fine high school teams seem like junior high squads. Few authorities doubted that the string and the dominance would end at this point. "Not since the days of the famous Franklin Wonder Five has any team been so pronounced a favorite to win the Indiana high school basketball championship as Crispus Attucks," pronounced Jep Cadou Jr. No one was foolish enough to disagree.[21]

Even the other coaches in the tournament sadly joined the consensus. In Indianapolis, at the Downtown Kiwanis Club's annual basketball banquet, they discussed their chances—or more precisely, lack of chances. "I'll have to predict Attucks to win," remarked Howard Sharpe of Terre Haute Gerstmeyer, whose team was scheduled to play the Tigers in the second afternoon contest. Marion Crawley of Lafayette Jefferson sought the refuge of abstract mathematics. "I'm just hoping the law of averages will take effect," he offered. Max Bell of Elkhart also discussed numbers, sagely commenting that the team that "gets the most points is usually the winner."[22]

Discussions of what team could defeat Attucks tended to circle toward home. Along the Avenue there was general agreement that the only team that would have a chance was the 1954–55 Tigers. Bill Hampton and Bill Scott were better shots than most of the 1955–56 Tigers, some claimed, and Willie Merriweather and Sheddrick Mitchell were powerful forces under the boards. But the 1955 championship star was Oscar, and in 1956 he was still the premier player and one year better. Now that was something to ponder—one year better than the best ever. For *Recorder* reporter Jim Cummings, however, one thing was certain: "Attucks's Tigers are still the jumpin'est, runnin'est, shootin'est and defensin'est team in the whole state." He predicted that at the final horn Attucks would be the first undefeated team in the history of the state to win the championship and would also possess the longest consecutive victory streak.[23]

A week of talking, predicting, and planning led to Saturday, March 17, a partly cloudy day that saw the temperatures climb into the low forties. The players from the four teams were ready. They had recovered from a flu bug that had "nipped" all the teams earlier in the week. In the first afternoon contest Lafayette and Elkhart battled for the entire game. Fourteen times the lead changed hands; twelve times the score was tied. With two minutes and forty-five seconds remaining in the game Elkhart led 50-48 with Lafayette center Vic Klinker at the foul line. Klinker missed, but Lafayette's leading scorer, Ronnie Fisher, snatched the rebound and shot, making the basket and getting fouled on the play. Then he missed the foul shot, and Klinker tapped it in, giving Lafayette a 52-50 lead. Both teams scored in the next minute and a half, and with time running out Lafayette controlled the ball and nursed a two-point lead. Elkhart then forced a turnover and called time-out, setting up a final shot. Elkhart got its chance when a reserve player drove off a pick toward the basket, but he penetrated too far and had to attempt an acrobatic shot that missed. Marion Crawley, one of the state's legendary coaches, advanced to the final game for the fifth time.[24]

The second game seemed less exciting, at least at first. Attucks had played Gerstmeyer in November, crushing the Terre Haute team 98-52. Perhaps that easy victory made the Tigers overconfident; perhaps they were a bit tight. Whatever the reason, from the opening tip Attucks played poorly, even as it controlled the game. The Tigers forced passes, fouled, and played as if they wanted to lose. But the fifteen thousand cheering spectators and the pressure of a state tournament game also overwhelmed the Gerstmeyer players. At the end of the first quarter Attucks led by seven points, and although it made only two of nine shots in the next period it still led by seven at the half. Attucks played better in the third quarter and extended its lead, but fouls continued to be a problem. With three minutes left in the period a referee whistled Robertson for his fourth foul. Wanting to protect Oscar for the final period, Crowe immediately sent Sam Milton to the scorers' table. Milton checked in and kneeled beside the court, but before there was a break in the game Oscar got his hands on the ball and dribbled into the chest of his defender. A referee's whistle froze both teams.[25]

The score was 47-35. Two minutes and six seconds remained in the third quarter, and Oscar Robertson was out of the game. Coach Sharpe and the Gerstmeyer bench were on their feet, cheering and shouting encouragement to their team. What was perhaps even more telling, a *Recorder* writer noted, "practically everyone outside the Tiger section applauded wildly." Oscar—"the magnificent Oscar Robertson"—was gone, and more than ten minutes remained in the game. The glorious winning streak, to say nothing of another state championship, was on the line.[26]

Crowe was worried. He admitted as much after the game. "Of course, I was a little concerned," he told reporters. But he also felt that "we're not a one-man ball club and we had a pretty good lead." In a brilliant tactical move, Crowe did nothing. He didn't overreact, he didn't order the team to stall, he didn't lose confidence in his players. And his Tigers responded to his calm faith in them. Bill Brown and Stanford Patton continued to dominate the boards, and underclassmen Edgar Searcy and Al Maxey hit crucial shots. Without Oscar, Attucks continued to play superbly. The closest Gerstmeyer could get was eight points, and Attucks won 68-59. "They're terrific," Sharpe said after the game.[27]

The final was set: the Lafayette Broncos versus the Crispus Attucks Tigers. "Before the season opened," Bob Collins reflected, "the big question was 'Who will beat Attucks?' As the season progressed it changed to 'Can anybody beat Attucks?' And finally, with the chaff culled and the tourney reaching the twilight stage for contenders, one formidable opponent stood and said, 'one thing for sure now, if we don't beat Attucks no one will.'" Certainly Lafayette had the coach to do the job. Basketball fans throughout the state called Marion Crawley the "Master." He had won three state titles—with Washington in 1941 and 1942 and with Lafayette in 1948—and seven times he had been in the final four, five times in the past nine years. Another title would tie him with legendary Everett Case and Glenn Curtis for the most state titles. And the inside-outside combination of Vic Klinker and Ronnie Fisher seemed to give Lafayette the necessary versatility.[28]

But few sportswriters really gave Lafayette much of a chance. Attucks, they agreed, was too tough. The Tigers had been ranked number one since November, they had played many of the finest teams in the state, and not once had they wilted under pressure. The reporters did, however, find an interesting story line: Oscar Robertson versus Ronnie Fisher for the state playoff scoring record. The year before, Wilson Eison of Gary Roosevelt had established a new mark with ninety-seven points in semifinal and final play. Fisher's twenty-one points against Elkhart put him just nineteen away from tying the record. Oscar's early departure against Gerstmeyer handicapped his chances. He needed thirty points to match Eison. If the game lived down to expectations, the scoring race might prove a more interesting drama.

No game had ever visibly and visually so marked an important transition. Two teams jogged onto the floor of Butler Fieldhouse on Saturday night, March 17, 1956. They warmed up and then formed a circle for the opening jump. Five players on one team, dressed in dark outfits, were all white; the other squad players, dressed in light outfits, were all black. Crispus

Attucks, the team with the black players and the light uniforms, won the tap. Taking the ball at center court, Oscar Robertson drove toward the top of the key, faked left, took a few quick dribbles to the right, then pulled up and hit a twelve-foot jumper. In nine seconds Attucks led 2-0, and the best high school player in the country had simply and economically announced his presence.

From a distance of years the contrast between the two teams is startling. The only preserved tape is grainy and silent, clearly a document from some bygone age. The pattern of Lafayette's play fits the film. The Broncos' play was Old School— or, perhaps, Ancient School. They played half-court, high-post basketball, using short two-handed chest passes to work the ball into their center. By the standards of the day they played their game well, patiently passing, probing for an opening, rationing out dribbles in spoonfuls, like precious water in a desert. On their second possession the Broncos threw thirty-four passes— and finally scored.

Had Lafayette been playing another two-handed-chest-passing, crew-cut-wearing high school team from the mid-1950s, it might have had a chance because it protected, shot, and re-bounded the ball well. But it had no defense for Attucks, a team that threw few passes and treated every offensive series as if it were something to finish as soon as possible. Attucks pushed the ball up the court, quickly got it into Robertson's hands, and waited for some happy result. Often Oscar simply took it to the hoop himself, seemingly oblivious of double and triple teams. On one sweet move early in the game he drove down the right side of the lane, discovered that he was trapped under the basket, and in one graceful, balletic move, stopped, reached back with his left hand, and massaged the ball into the basket.

Years later Lafayette's Vic Klinker still recalled the frustration of playing against Robertson. "Attucks had a fine bunch of players, but they were no better than we were. Oscar was the difference. And there was nothing we could do to stop [him]. We tried four different players on him. Nothing." In fact, Klinker was the only starter who did not get a shot at covering Oscar. "I like to think that it was because the coach didn't want me to foul out, but that's just a story I tell now. The truth is that no one could cover Oscar. He was just too good."

The pace of the game resembled a kid playing with a faucet—a burst of water followed by a trickle giving way to a torrent and then another slow drip, drip, drip. Midway through the first period the Tigers solved the riddle of the Lafayette offense. Playing a matchup zone defense, they trapped the ball when it was passed into the corners and forced the Broncos to shoot faster, seemingly unconcerned if the ball went in or not. The idea was that a fast-paced game ultimately favored Attucks. By contrast, Lafayette could not slow down Attucks's offense or keep the Tigers from getting second and third shots. At the end of the first quarter Attucks led 20-11, and the game had entered into an uncompetitive phase. Both teams would still try and play fine basketball, but Lafayette seemed out of the game.

The spectators sat stunned, almost as if they were seeing something they had never seen and never even imagined. Attucks "was so good," commented Bob Collins of the *Indianapolis Star,* "most of the huge crowd in Butler Fieldhouse forgot to root against the favorite—as is the custom—soon after the game opened and spent the evening staring, open-mouthed, at the effortless way the Tigers reduced this game of basketball to its primary form— putting the ball in the basket." After watching Oscar and his team struggle in the afternoon game, many spectators, especially Lafayette fans, had allowed themselves to entertain slim hopes of success. But that evening they saw Oscar in his full glory, and their reaction, according to Collins, could be summarized in a single word: "wow!!"[29]

Playing his last game for Attucks, Oscar was determined to prove he was the finest basketball player in Indiana. Sometimes it even seemed that he was competing against the ghosts of players past. He connected on powerful drives to the basket and on large arching set shots, on pull-up jump shots from his favorite spots and on turnaround fadeaways from the block. On one memorable play in the third quarter he drove across the lane from left to right and banked in a sweeping hook shot that "brought a gasp from the crowd." Whenever Lafayette threatened to get the game close enough to make a serious run, Oscar responded with a shot or an assist to move the game back to a safe, noncompetitive level. And with a nice touch of the artistically dramatic, he saved his best for last, scoring seventeen points in the fourth quarter and ending with a series of twenty- to thirty-foot set shots. He finished with thirty-nine points, breaking Dee Monroe's thirty-six-point record for a final game and Wilson Eison's ninety-seven-point semifinal and final tournament mark. "That Oscar Robertson is the greatest high school player I have seen in all my years of coaching," Marion Crawley said after the game. "He'll kill you anywhere because he can do anything. . . . There just isn't any way to stop him."[30]

In the end, Lafayette played well, shooting more than 40 percent and committing only four turnovers. Yet Attucks hardly noticed. The Tigers shot better and committed even fewer errors, but the game was never about percentages and numbers. It was about style—old versus new, even white versus black. The Lafayette brand of basketball belonged to the Indiana of the past, a state of small towns and small farms. Attucks's game came from the soul of America's urban ghettos, from places like the Dust

Bowl, where black youths played their city game. As practiced by Oscar Robertson, it was not exactly flashy; Oscar didn't sky, and Oscar didn't fly. Writer Nelson George compared Oscar's game to the music of Nat King Cole, "a smooth, understated, yet swinging vocalist who blended the crooning big-band singing tradition with the slick blues he played as a pianist. Robertson did everything the classroom coaches loved; he just did all of it better than anyone else ever had." But in one detail—the most important detail—he linked the early blacktop game with the later, more explosive one. Oscar was a relentless, aggressive, in-your-face offensive force. He wasn't coy, and he didn't beat around the bush. He pushed the ball forward and seemed to challenge—even threaten—defenders to stop him. That, in the end, was what Oscar's game was all about—drive, excellence, and confidence.[31]

Oscar's desire had infected his teammates, giving them the confidence—the sense of destiny—to achieve the previously unachievable. They had done it. No team had ever gone undefeated through a season in Indiana basketball. In 1935 Jeffersonville had made it to the final game without a loss but then had fallen to Anderson 23-17. Though the teams and scores were different in 1947, the same scenario was played out again. That time Shelbyville trounced a previously unbeaten Terre Haute Garfield. But now after forty-six years of tournament competition that oddity was no more. Just as the year before an all-black team from Crispus Attucks had ended Indianapolis's weary tradition of tournament futility, now another all-black squad from the same school had walked into history. In two years Crispus Attucks had won two state championships and sixty-one games, and it had lost only once. And it had a streak of forty-five games to pass on to the next year's team.

But no one thought much of looking ahead. Now it was time to celebrate, time to hug and laugh and let the feelings of pure joy out onto the floor of Butler Fieldhouse. When the game ended, the game faces went with it. Oscar jumped in the air, landing near the Attucks bench where teammates reached to embrace him. "State, Man!" shouted tiny Lavern Benson as he grabbed one teammate and then another. Coach Crowe, normally reserved and always poised in public, accepted congratulations from everyone close enough to shake his hand or slap his back. "Thanks, thanks," he mumbled over and over as tears formed in the corners of his eyes. In six years as head coach he had reached the summit of Indiana high school basketball—two state titles and a win-loss record of 154-14. There were rumors before the contest that this would be his last game, rumors that he would depart coaching to devote his energies to an insurance company or perhaps even follow Oscar to the college ranks. For the moment, however, all those thoughts belonged to another place. Embracing Oscar, his mind was blank and his emotions were overflowing.[32]

The celebrations continued as Crowe and his players accepted gold-plated championship rings and the big championship trophy, which they passed around, kissing the gold basketball on the top. Players that pushed so hard on the court now took their time, chatting with newspaper and television reporters, posing for countless photographs, discussing the game with friends. Eventually they turned to the ritual of cutting down the net, then they sauntered toward their dressing room, loud with laughter and talk. Seriousness had dominated the dressing room after sectional, regional, and semifinal action; they had all been earnest young men intent on taking care of business. But with that business sweetly dispatched, the players had turned into blissful Alexanders, conquerors of worlds with gold rings on their hands and smiles on their faces. "State, Man," Benson continued like a record that kept skipping at the best spot. "State, Man."[33]

From the dressing room they left the fieldhouse and boarded a fire truck. The players were now quiet, but sirens, fire bells, horns, and "superhuman" cheers filled the crisp night air. It was a scene out of an A. E. Housman poem:

> *The time you won your town the race*
> *We chaired you through the market-place;*
> *Men and boy stood cheering by,*
> *And home we brought you shoulder-high.*[34]

On wheels the din headed east and then south, the players' fire truck sandwiched between half a dozen police motorcycles and another fire truck alive with cheerleaders and reporters. A mile-long motorcade filled with cheering people trailed the lead vehicles down Meridian Street, past the governor's mansion, whose lights blinked in salute, and on to Monument Circle. The stop at the Circle was as brief as the one the year before, just long enough for Oscar to jump from the truck, scale the monument's south steps, and greet the crowd with a wave. Then the wheels started to turn again, traveling from Indiana Avenue to the Northwestern Community Center, where fuel for a bonfire stood patiently waiting.[35]

Someone in some official capacity lit the bonfire while happy Attucks fans danced on the grass and tennis courts.

"Is this the greatest team in the 40-year history of this riotous tournament?" sportswriter Jep Cadou Jr. asked the next morning. "Who is to say? Hoosiers will be arguing that point long into the night for many years." Cadou's question—and his evasive answer—was typical of how most white sportswriters and reporters translated the success of the Crispus Attucks Tigers.

For them it was not just primarily a sports story, it was exclusively a sports story, and they trafficked in numbers and opinions. Two consecutive state titles, four consecutive sectional and regional titles, forty-five consecutive victories, the most points in a regular-season game and a regional-tournament game—these were the statistics that the sportswriters used to quantify success and measure greatness. They employed the same yardstick to pass judgment on Oscar Robertson—most points in a single game, most points in a regular season, most points in a career, most points in a title game. One statistic piled on another as if numbers were the only thing that mattered, as if the sum of the accomplishments of Oscar and his teammates were jottings on a ledger sheet.[36]

But the numbers tell only part of the story and the least important part at that. Just as the statistics generated by the Montgomery Bus Boycott—the decline in bus traffic, the lost revenue—could not measure the meaning of what was taking place in that southern city, so the tabulations of basketball games could not properly gauge the meaning of the Crispus Attucks Tigers. From the first—from even before construction began on the school—it was a story about race and power. The very existence of Crispus Attucks High School announced where the power was in Indianapolis. It said, loudly, that white citizens had the cultural, political, and economic muscle to bar black children from going to school with white children. It said, also loudly, that white was superior, black was inferior, and that was just the way it was. These same attitudes and notions soon became part of the common currency in sports. White teams won titles, white players were more competitive, white coaches were smarter—and that was just the way it was.

Crispus Attucks challenged the myths and made people think differently. Like the Montgomery Bus Boycott, the Tigers targeted the racial status quo by refusing to believe that that was just how it was. The Tigers were in the forefront of the movement athletically, but not by much. Other all-black high schools—Miller in Detroit, Lockland Wayne near Cincinnati, Dunbar and DuSable in Illinois—were also competing successfully, and black players like Bill Russell and K. C. Jones were dominating college basketball. The "ba-ad, ba-a-ad Tigers" showed all of Indiana that at least on the basketball court times were changing and old racial notions were dead. On the court they played with joy, energy, and a sense of freedom, boundless and infectious.[37]

The problem was that the freedom and success on a basketball court did not translate well into the rest of society. "When Do We Celebrate?" asked a headline on the front page of the *Indianapolis Recorder*. The writer knew that many Indianapolis residents resented Attucks for no other reason than it was an all-black team, and in the postgame celebrations he saw the racism that was part of everyday life. Attucks's triumph, he said, was a community one, but the celebrations, the bonfire, and the joy were confined to the west side of the city. Downtown storefronts carried no best-wishes signs, and during the celebrations city police discouraged "whites from journeying into Negro sections." The newspaper asked: "When is Indianapolis—all of Indianapolis—going to raise a loud, clear voice in at least a gesture of appreciation of the wonderful things the Tigers hav[e] done for this city?"[38]

Black writers had a greater sense than white journalists of what the Crispus Attucks Tigers represented. "Every American Negro consciously able to take a breath should care" about the Tigers, commented one black editorialist. The undefeated season "is glorious enough, but its implications concerning the entire picture of racial segregation are of absolutely world-shaking importance. It is not illogical to suppose that, if such a great team was potentially present all along and secreted only because of senseless discrimination, similar greatness is potentially present in other fields. The Attucks T[i]gers, in other words, help back up the Negro's cry, 'Give me a chance. I'll prove my worth!'" In an age of bus boycotts, school desegregation, and protest marches, basketball had become a symbolic drama, a ruler to measure how far African Americans had come and a crystal ball to predict how far they might go.[39]

"There is a danger present, however," warned the editorialist. "The American Negro, perhaps through years of enjoying the niceties of life only as a spectator, has a remarkable ability to bask vicariously in another's glory. There are people walking every street today who fail to achieve their own God-given glory, partly because of discrimination from the outside, but also because of lack of application inside." Ray Crowe's Tigers, however, offered an alternative. They won not just because they were given a chance but because of "hard, grueling work and self-sacrificing teamwork." In searching for the ultimate meaning of the Tigers, the *Recorder* managed to weld together liberal and conservative racial philosophies, the activism of the NAACP with the self-help teachings of Booker T. Washington. Convinced that true racial advancement depended on both equal access to opportunity and individual drive, the editorialist discovered in a basketball championship a formula for life.[40]

END GAMES

Branch McCracken must have known that Oscar Robertson was perfect for his brand of basketball. When he had replaced his mentor and coach Everett Dean as head coach of Indiana University in 1938, he had radically altered the way the game was played not only at IU but across the entire state. Dean's offense centered on a ball-control, four-man weave. If not entirely slow, the disciplined style had a leaden, narcotic aspect. McCracken gave the program wings. Like other coaches of the period he fell under the spell of the fast-break offense. In its classic form the fast break began with a rebounder who made a quick release pass to an outlet man. The idea was to gain an immediate numerical advantage (usually three against two), fill the lanes, move rapidly down the court employing the pass, and finish with a layup.

Some Indiana players believed that McCracken liked his system more than he liked his players. Throughout the late 1930s and the 1940s he angrily watched other states drain Indiana of its best high school talent. In 1938 seven of the ten members of the University of Southern California Trojans were Hoosier high school products; in fact, in a game against the University of California, the Berkeley band greeted the USC players with "(Back Home Again in) Indiana." One early-1940s Michigan State team boasted five Indiana starters. Everett Case, a Hoosier himself, built championship teams at North Carolina State with Indiana high school graduates. In 1948 high school all-star Clyde Lovellette shocked the state when he left Indiana for the University of Kansas, where he became the key player on a national championship team. Another Indiana player, who took his talents to Vanderbilt, recalled a game against the University of Mississippi where twelve of the twenty players were raised within fifty miles of each other in southern Indiana. "It was like a homecoming," he said.[1]

But the worst thief was Adolph Rupp of the University of Kentucky. His greatest sin, in Hoosiers' minds, was not so much that he stole some of the best Indiana players but that he bragged about it. At a time when Rupp's distinctive jowls were just beginning to inch toward his collar, he observed that there was nothing sacrosanct about the Ohio River and that the soil above it was pretty much the same as the soil below. Finally, McCracken had had enough, announcing that he planned to recruit only five players a year—the five best Indiana players—and the rest of the country could have the table scraps. As something akin to a patriotic duty, he asked the Indiana high school coaches to help him identify and recruit the five best.[2]

By the 1950s McCracken's plan was well in place. A statewide network of clinics taught the "McCracken system" to high school coaches who in turn schooled their wards in fast-break basketball and funneled the very best to IU. In 1953 Indiana won the Big Ten and NCAA championships. Led by all-Americans Bob Leonard and Don Schlundt, every player on that Indiana team had graduated from a Hoosier high school.[3]

In the mid-1950s, however, the constant recruiting wars had begun to wear on McCracken. By that time—and probably long before—some of the best players were being paid to attend school. In the winter of 1954–55 Wilt Chamberlain of Philadelphia's Overbrook High School set off a recruiting war. More than two hundred schools approached him, many with bids in excess of the standard athletic scholarship. "I had offers from damn near every state in the union—plus Hawaii, which wasn't even a state yet," Chamberlain recalled. "Alphabetically, the schools ranged from Arizona State to Xavier of Ohio." Indiana was one of the three or four schools on Chamberlain's short list, but the black center heard "disturbing rumors that McCracken wasn't all that fond of blacks," and although he was told that IU would double whatever he was offered at his other choices, he decided to attend Kansas.[4]

Indiana might have been outbid, although McCracken would later tell a different story. He charged that Chamberlain had been offered to him for five thousand dollars up front, but that he had refused to pay. "We thought we had Wilt," he told a reporter. "He was announced for here. Phog [Forrest Allen] stole him away from us. I didn't mind losing him so much as I minded losing him to Allen." If there was anyone McCracken disliked more than Rupp it was Kansas's Allen, whose team Indiana had defeated in the 1953 NCAA finals.

Allen luxuriated in his Chamberlain sweepstakes triumph. As Allen recalled his campaign to sign Chamberlain, "The people in Kansas wanted another Jackie Robinson. And they wanted to win. Wilt was a way to kill two birds with one stone. I wanted to win. I didn't care about another Jackie Robinson. I played every angle I could think of to get him. One was to have the Negro talk to the Negro. I brought in colored leaders from our community to pitch to him." Allen personally sold Wilt's mother on the value of a Kansas degree—"Mamas like to believe they are thinking more about education than about basketball"—and made sure Chamberlain received royal treatment during his three visits to Kansas. "I rolled out the red carpet every time Wilt came to town," Allen recalled. "I shot every barrel. I not only landed my prey, but I had the pleasure of seeing some of the fall-out wound good old IU and my good friend, Branch McCracken."

Chamberlain admitted that he and his mother liked Allen, but he felt the cash was more important than a new friendship. Exactly how much Wilt "earned" at Kansas remains a bit fuzzy. After all, payoffs seldom generate precise tax returns. For the record, Chamberlain told the NCAA, the FBI, and the IRS that the scholarship he accepted from Kansas included tuition, room, board, and $15 a month for laundry and incidentals. When his playing career ended, he admitted that friends of the Kansas program had sweetened the pot. He recalled that he got spending money whenever he needed it, perhaps as much as $15,000 to $20,000 during his two years of varsity basketball. He also received a Cadillac, an automobile that eventually put Kansas on NCAA probation. As far as Chamberlain was concerned, accepting the money, however illegally, was just good business. His presence on the court generated millions of dollars for the university, the city of Lawrence, and the state. With Wilt in a Kansas uniform, local business was very, very good. "Why should I let them exploit me, without reaping at least a little of the profit myself?" he wondered. "I figured it was a fair trade."[5]

If reporters, investigators, and coaches at other schools did not know the exact figures of the Chamberlain deal, they had no doubt that the price was high. While most reporters condemned the corruption of college athletics, Leonard Lewin of the *New York Daily News* expressed concern for Chamberlain: "I feel sorry for the Stilt when he enters the NBA. . . . He'll have to take a cut in salary."

Undoubtedly, the Chamberlain fiasco was still fresh in McCracken's mind, the bitter loss to Allen still smarting, when he cautiously began to recruit Robertson. Another black player, another angle, he guessed. But Oscar's game was made for McCracken's offense. He could rebound like a forward and pass and dribble like a guard. He was perhaps the only player who could play every position in the offense, and he could outrun every member of IU's team. McCracken must have known this; his assistant coaches, scouts, and informal bird dogs must have told him. If nothing else, his players might have told him. Oscar had played on a team in summer tournaments that had defeated a team with Schlundt and several other IU players.

And in Robertson, McCracken had a willing recruit. He was not then or ever a Wilt Chamberlain. Chamberlain was brash, streetwise, and outgoing, almost prematurely hardened in the ways of commerce. Oscar was reserved, remarkably innocent, and serious. Seventy-five or more schools expressed an interest in him, but unlike Chamberlain he never counted the letters. He demonstrated an almost total lack of interest in visiting all but a few campuses, and he was not particularly eager for free trips, free food, free entertainment, or free women. Even the recruiters' telephone calls were a nuisance. Frequently he slept at his father's house to escape the calls, and three times his father had his own phone disconnected. As Oscar's senior year neared completion he was really interested in only IU.[6]

Part of Oscar's ambivalence about the recruitment process was that he did not fully understand how it worked. It was really part of that other world—the white world—filled with white people, big promises, and potential problems. Several of his friends had already been through the ordeal, and they had told Oscar enough to make him wary. Herschell Turner, who was planning to graduate from Shortridge in 1956, had recently gone to Michigan State on a recruiting trip with only a few bucks in his pocket and returned with a hundred dollars. When he showed it to his mother, she made him send it back, remarking, "They can't buy you." "She thought it was a slave thing," Oscar recalled. On another trip, Turner had taken a plane to Nebraska. His mother had given him five dollars. Unsure of the price of food on planes, he had asked the stewardess how much a couple of hot dogs cost. "No one told him about such things," said Oscar. "We didn't know about planes and such. That's not how we traveled. It was not part of our universe."

Bill Scott had also run into problems in college. He had gone to Franklin College, a small institution in south-central Indiana. Accustomed to the competition at Attucks and the playgrounds of black Indianapolis, he discovered that he was a "big pea" at Franklin. The first game he played he scored thirty-nine points, and he scored thirty-three in the second. But he was the only black on the squad, and his teammates, who were also fraternity brothers, told the coach they felt they could play better without him. In Scott's third game he sat on the bench for the first half and watched his team struggle. Down by six, his coach made a change in the lineup. "I started the second half, scored twenty-seven points, and we won the game. But the next game, the coach said, 'These guys still think that they can play better without you.'" Scott was in a no-win situation; the better he played the more his teammates resented him. Finally he quit the team and transferred to another school.

Oscar knew the Turner and Scott stories, but he thought IU might be different. For one thing, he was familiar with the school. He made the short trip down Highway 37 to Bloomington dozens of times to visit Attucks friends who had gone to IU. He liked what he saw of the small town and wooded campus, so different in almost every way from his Indianapolis neighborhood, but in a comfortable way oddly similar. He spent nights in a particularly close friend's room, talking about basketball and life and the subjects that interested teenagers. By the time track season was over and he was allowed to make official campus visits, he was ready to select Indiana. All he needed was an invitation.

One spring day Coach Crowe drove Oscar to Bloomington to meet with McCracken. McCracken, however, was not prepared to woo the premier player in the country, or perhaps he had just decided to play hardball. He kept player and coach waiting outside his office for forty-five minutes before inviting them inside. Then, quiet for a moment, he looked at Robertson, perhaps trying to gauge the man in the teenager. If so, his attempt was a singular failure. "I hope you're not the kind of kid who wants money to go to school," he began.

Wrong opening. McCracken had uttered only one sentence, but Oscar had heard enough. He knew that what he had heard about McCracken's attitude about black players was true. He knew that the terrible stories he had heard about Hallie Bryant's time at IU were true. The coach's words stung Oscar badly. They insulted, embarrassed, and angered him. He was an innocent kid from a sheltered, religious background who knew little about above-the-table handshakes and under-the-table payoffs. The players he knew from Attucks who had received scholarships to colleges had not been given money, and he did not know well very many players outside of Attucks. He was shy, and he was accustomed to decent treatment from his coaches and the adults he respected. Now here was this white coach with a southern accent and a brusque manner virtually accusing him of soliciting money to attend IU.

"Coach, I got to leave," Oscar told Crowe as he walked out of McCracken's office. That was it, just "I got to leave." Nearly a half century later Oscar Robertson still felt the pain of that moment. "If [McCracken] had said, 'Oscar, we would like you to come to Indiana and play basketball for us,' I would have said, 'Fine, where do I sign?' But I never did anything to deserve the treatment I got." One thing he was certain of then and later: "I did not like Branch McCracken. Branch McCracken did not like black people. There was no way I would go to IU and play for him."

But if not Indiana, where? Purdue University, sixty miles to the northwest, seemed as distant culturally as IU. With a mostly white student body, surrounded by patches of flat, rich farm-land, it was an IU without nearly as many trees, the rolling land-scape, or the limestone buildings. But Ray Eddy, Purdue's coach, was developing a reputation for aggressively recruiting black play-ers. During the 1955–56 season, Lamar Lundy, an all-American football player and center on the basketball team, was one of the leaders of the squad. He would be joined on the 1956–57 team by a group of talented black sophomores, including 1955 Indi-ana Mr. Basketball Wilson Eison, Willie Merriweather, Harvey Austin, and Charlie Lyons.

But the number of black players on Purdue's team both-ered Robertson. He had played with and against most of them, knew their games well, and suspected that some were spending time on the bench watching less talented white players start and play. The reason was obvious: the quota system. Most, if not all, major schools that recruited black players observed a quota on how many blacks they could have on the court at any one time. Glenn Sample, a longtime fixture in the University of Cincinnati athletic program, observed that the rule was simple: "Two at home, three on the road, four if you needed the game."

Oscar was not concerned about being a victim of the system—he had confidence in his own abilities—but he knew that if he went to Purdue he would probably bump a black player from the starting lineup, and that was not something he wanted to do. In addition he sensed that Purdue was not right for him. Growing up in a black urban environment and attending all-black schools, he was unaccustomed to the nearly all-white Purdue student body. He did not resent Purdue or dislike the coach, he just did not feel the school was right for him.

The only other Big Ten school he visited was Michigan. Perhaps "visit" is the wrong word because he did not actually make it to the campus. Shortly after visiting IU and Purdue, he flew to Detroit. It was his first time in an airplane, and he was nervous. No one greeted him when he reached the terminal, so he waited a half hour before calling the coach. The Michigan staff members had forgotten about his visit, and he promptly forgot about them, returning to Indianapolis on the next flight.

By then the novelty of the recruitment process had worn thin. John Wooden at UCLA tried to get Robertson to visit the West Coast, but Oscar refused. He recalled thinking, "Go to California? Jesus Christ, I'd have to fly on an airplane for three, four, five, maybe seven hours. Stop eight times." Unlike Chamberlain, he had no desire to go to school far from home, and a seven-hour flight seemed a steep price to pay for a few free meals and a lonely hotel room.

In the end it came down to one school: the University of Cincinnati. Without really investigating or knowing much about the university, Cincinnati seemed like a good school for Robertson. Cincinnati, two hours or so south of Indianapolis on Highway 52, was a midsize, racially mixed city, not terribly different from Indianapolis. Oscar had been there several times to watch Jackie Robinson's Brooklyn Dodgers play the Cincinnati

Reds. Sitting in the segregated bleachers at Crosley Field, he had been surrounded by friendly black faces. Oscar's memories of games at Crosley Field differ from those of other blacks. Many blacks recall the hostile racial vibes of Reds fans dragged up from Kentucky and West Virginia, racial slurs that seemed to shatter the moments of silence, and the 1952 death threat against Jackie Robinson that necessitated armed bodyguards. "The worst fans were in Cincinnati," recalled one black player. "Whenever there was a lull, some loudmouth would yell: 'Nigger' or 'black unprintable' and you could hear it all over the place."[7]

Oscar remembered not the segregated stands—he did not even notice them—but the general joy of the spectators who surrounded him. For many people, watching Jackie Robinson was like a religious experience, fulfilling, giving joy and hope and a sense of well-being. That in itself was enough to give Cincinnati a warm glow.

Cincinnati basketball coach George Smith labored to sustain that feeling. Smith had grown up on an Ohio farm and had a pleasant down-home quality, a sort of aw-shucks style that put people at ease. "Parents liked George," said Glenn Sample, one of his close friends. "He could recruit mothers—convince them that he would take real good care of their sons. And he did. George did not have any children of his own, and his players became part of his family." Smith and the University of Cincinnati had another competitive advantage: money, or more specifically, untainted money. In 1906 the university started the first "cooperative system" in the United States, a model for other such programs. By the mid-1950s more than three thousand of the university's students were in the co-op system, alternating quarters of study with quarters of work. The school arranged the jobs, and the jobs paid as much as ninety or one hundred dollars a week. Co-op employment, coupled with a standard athletic scholarship, offered Oscar something more than student poverty.[8]

When Oscar visited Cincinnati, Smith introduced him to several of the town's leading black and white businessmen and politicians, men singled out to impress the high school senior. Ted Berry, who would become Cincinnati's first black mayor, showed Oscar around the town, and Ross Hastings, a wealthy friend of the university and the basketball team, invited Robertson and his teammate Al Maxey to his home. Cultures clashed. For two west-side youths whose idea of money was a few dollars in their pockets, Hastings's home seemed a product of another universe. In his backyard were a pool, tennis court, and basketball court, as well as chairs for lounging and tables for eating. Robertson and Maxey looked at each other and mouthed a silent "wow!"

Oscar mostly just looked and listened. "I knew nothing about finance or culture or international relations," he remembered. "What could I possibly add to any conversation?" At one point, however, Hastings's young son drew a few words from Oscar when he chose a pause in a conversation to innocently observe, "Gee, you sure are black." "It got quiet. I mean *really* quiet," Oscar remembered. "They probably thought I was going to snatch the kid and choke him." But Oscar just smiled and explained that his ancestors were from another continent where it was very hot and dark skin was the norm.

The time Oscar spent in Cincinnati was pleasant enough, even if there were a few awkward moments. His hosts meant well, and in their warm, generous manner they worked to put him at ease. It was the questions he did not know to ask, the signals that he did not know to look for, that passed unanswered and unobserved. He was already impressed with UC's fine business school and co-op program, but he failed to inquire if the school or sports program had an equally good record for placing black graduates. And he never noticed that during his recruitment trip he seldom spent much time at the university itself. He saw the best side of Cincinnati, met the nicest people, and never asked if there was anything else.

Robertson officially announced his decision to attend Cincinnati on June 9, 1956, the day after his high school graduation ceremonies. He graduated in the upper tenth of his class, sixteenth out of 171. But he still had two games left in his Indiana basketball career.[9]

In Indiana in the 1950s only a state championship game carried more prestige. A state championship was about a team and a town, one high school rising above hundreds of others. But in the Indiana-Kentucky Blind Fund Classic, two basketball-proud states scrapped for bragging rights. The best Indiana high school players versus the finest from Kentucky. For the players themselves, the honor of making the team was the final and most coveted one in their high school careers. Don Bates, a former director of the game, came closest to defining the meaning of being named to the Indiana all-star team: "When you die, that's in your obit, that you were an Indiana all-star. And it's usually in the lead paragraph."

The *Indianapolis Star* initiated the contest in 1940, and over the years the event has generated millions of dollars for charity. For the first fifteen years the game was played in Butler Fieldhouse, and Indiana benefited from the home-court advantage. Kentucky managed only one victory during those years; in the closing days of World War II, Wallace "Wah Wah" Jones and Ralph Beard, who would later help the University of Kentucky win a national championship, starred in the win. In 1955 two decisions reduced Indiana's supremacy. The sponsors agreed to play two games each year on a home-and-home basis, and Kentucky finally began to name black players to its squad.[10]

The 1956 reporters billed the contest as a battle between Oscar Robertson and "King" Kelly Coleman, who had scored 4,263 points in his record-breaking Wayland, Kentucky, high school career. Both had been selected as all-Americans—it was Oscar's second time on the list. And the two presented a nice contrast: Robertson, a soft-spoken product of a ghetto; Coleman, a wise-cracking, cowlicked country boy from the Kentucky hills. That line was fine for Coleman, although he suggested that a more interesting story might be his personal battle against the clock. Would he succeed in scoring 50 or more points in each game? He glibly asserted that he would. He had averaged more than 46 points a game during his senior year at Wayland, and he was certain that a bunch of Hoosier players could not guard him. Arriving for practice late, he told reporters, "I didn't think I needed any practice for Indiana."[11]

The Indiana team approached the contest less cavalierly, and most felt that if Coleman's comment was an attempt at humor, it was not funny. Over steaks at the 500 Club one evening before the first game, Coach Angus Nicoson asked, "Who wants to guard Kelly Coleman Saturday?" Several hands shot up. At the end of the table the normally reserved Oscar Robertson spoke: "Sorry boys, he's all mine."[12]

More than 14,500 people, the most ever to see an Indiana-Kentucky game, crammed into the stifling Butler Fieldhouse to watch the Robertson-Coleman duel. With shirts stuck wet to their backs, they cheered the action. Kentucky started fast, scoring the first seven points. Then Robertson led his team's comeback. He tied the score at 10-10 with more than five minutes left in the first quarter. Indiana then took a 12-10 lead and never lost it, winning 92-78. Whenever Kentucky threatened to make it a close game, Oscar hit a shot or set up another player. He finished with thirty-four points, breaking the single-game scoring record by six points. Sportswriter Bob Collins had seen Oscar play dozens of times, and he was seldom disappointed. "Oscar Robertson was never better (and that's very good indeed)," he wrote.[13]

In the locker room after the game, Kentucky coach Ted Hornback shook his head as he told a group of reporters that Oscar had turned what should have been a tight game into a mismatch. "He's a pro playing with a bunch of high school boys," Hornback explained. "He's the best high school basketball player I ever saw and better than a lot of college boys." Most everyone agreed. Robertson became the first player in the history of the series to claim the "Triple Crown": he was named Mr. Basketball, elected captain by his teammates, and chosen Star of Stars. Of the 108 sportswriters who voted for the Star of Stars, 106 named Oscar; the other two were blinded by hometown loyalties.[14]

Coleman underwhelmed the spectators. Both he and Oscar wore the traditional Mr. Basketball number one on their jerseys, but Coleman should have added a fraction after his number. Before the opening tap, Oscar shook hands with Coleman, then when the game began said, "OK, let's see what you got. Start scoring." Tightly guarding the Kentucky player, Oscar worked to deny him the ball and crowded his shots. Coleman scored only three points in the first half with Oscar covering him and finished with seventeen, most coming in the last quarter, after the game had been decided.

On Sunday the teams traveled to Louisville for their Monday-night game. Kentucky players talked about revenge, and reporters noted the previous year's 86-82 Kentucky victory in overtime. Kentuckians had long argued that they would do "terrible things" to Indiana once they got the game below the Ohio River, but by now everyone agreed that Oscar had the ability to nullify any home-court advantage.[15]

Unlike the first game, both teams started fast. Coach Nicoson believed the taller Kentucky team was slow and out of shape and told Oscar to keep pushing the ball up the court. The heat in the steaming Louisville Armory aided the Indiana cause. Until well into the third quarter, the teams raced back and forth. Ed Smallwood, one of the few black players on his team, helped Kentucky gain several first-half leads, although Indiana held a 47-46 halftime advantage. In the third quarter Kentucky recaptured the lead. Then, as so often had happened in Crispus Attucks games, Oscar simply took over. He tied the game with two free throws, distributed an assist, hit a jump shot, then stole the ball and drove in for another basket. Indiana led 59-53, and Kentucky faded. The Hoosier team scored thirty points in the third quarter and was up by nineteen.[16]

That left the fourth quarter for records. Midway through the quarter Robertson broke his own thirty-four-point scoring record with a rare four-point play. Indiana supporters cheered for a hundred-point game, but with Robertson on the bench their team missed several opportunities. Nicoson sent Oscar back in the game, and Oscar promptly made the hundred-point shot, only to be taken out to a standing ovation. But he had only a few seconds' rest. Someone told Nicoson that Oscar had thirty-nine points. With nine seconds remaining Nicoson signaled time-out.

"Do you think you could get another basket?" he asked Robertson.

"I can if I can get the ball," Oscar answered.[17]

He did and he did, making the last shot of his high school career. Indiana won 102-77, but Oscar's performance was the major story. "If there is anyone who doubts now that Oscar Robertson is the best high school basketball player in the world, he is speaking in very faint tones," wrote Bob Collins. Both Adolph Rupp and Branch McCracken, sitting at the press table, agreed. Robertson made seventeen of thirty-three field-goal attempts and seven of eight free throws. He controlled the game at both ends of the court, seemingly without real effort, and was once again named Indiana Star of Stars.[18]

By the end of the game most people had almost forgotten about Kelly Coleman's earlier prediction. In the second game the "greatest shooter in the country" made only one of nine shots and finished with four points. Afterward Coleman attempted to squirm out from under his incendiary remark. "With a gimpy leg and this," he said patting his ample belly, "I would be crazy to make the statements they said I did. . . . I realize that story about me scoring 50 points in each game sold tickets for the Blind Fund. But it made me look like a nitwit." Sensing an ugly embarrassment, he scrambled the best he could. He really had a bum leg, he said, and he was out of shape, and besides, the Kentucky players had never been known for their defensive abilities. But excuses aside, he said, "I never realized there could be so much difference between Indiana and Kentucky basketball."[19]

Then, almost as if he suddenly realized what made Indiana so much better, he added, "That Oscar is terrific."

Notes

PROLOGUE

1. For details of the game see *Indianapolis Recorder,* Mar. 10, 1951; *Indianapolis Star,* Mar. 4, 1951; Phillip M. Hoose, *Hoosiers: The Fabulous Basketball Life of Indiana,* 2d ed. (Indianapolis: Guild Press of Indiana, 1995), 160–69.

2. Kerry D. Marshall, *The Ray Crowe Story: A Legend in High School Basketball* ([Indianapolis]: High School Basketball Cards of America, 1992), 44; *Indianapolis Recorder,* Mar. 10, 1951.

3. *Indianapolis Star,* Mar. 4, 1951.

4. Ibid., Mar. 5, 1951.

5. *Indianapolis Recorder,* Mar. 10, 1951.

6. *Indianapolis Star,* Mar. 4, 1951.

7. *Indianapolis Recorder,* Mar. 10, 1951; *Indianapolis Star,* Mar. 4, 1951; Hoose, *Hoosiers,* 166.

8. For a history of the scandals see Charles Rosen, *Scandals of '51: How Gamblers Almost Killed College Basketball* (New York: Holt, Rinehart and Winston, 1978); Stanley Cohen, *The Game They Played* (New York: Farrar, Straus and Giroux, 1977); Randy Roberts and James S. Olson, *Winning Is the*

Only Thing: Sports in America since 1945 (Baltimore: Johns Hopkins University Press, 1989), 73–92.

9.   Roberts and Olson, *Winning Is the Only Thing*, 84.

10.   *Indianapolis Star*, Mar. 4, 1951.

11.   Ibid., Mar. 11, 1951; *Indianapolis Recorder*, Mar. 17, 1951.

12.   *Indianapolis Star*, Mar. 11, 1951; *Indianapolis Recorder*, Mar. 17, 1951.

13.   *Indianapolis Recorder*, Mar. 17, 1951.

14.   Ibid.

15.   Ibid.

16.   Marshall, *Ray Crowe Story*, 44.

17.   Hoose, *Hoosiers*, 167.

18.   *Indianapolis Star*, Mar. 18, 1951; *Indianapolis Recorder*, Mar. 24, 1951.

19.   Hoose, *Hoosiers*, 168.

CHAPTER ONE

1.   *Cincinnati Enquirer*, Jan. 5, 1959.

2.   Langston Hughes, "Bound No'th Blues," in *Fine Clothes to the Jew* (New York: Alfred A. Knopf, 1927), 87; Jay R. Mandle, *Not Slave, Not Free: The African American Economic Experience since the Civil War* (Durham, N.C.: Duke University Press, 1992), 42–43.

3.   Nicholas Lemann, *The Promised Land: The Great Black Migration and How It Changed America* (New York: Alfred A. Knopf, 1991), 17–19.

4.   Carter G. Woodson, "The Exodus during the World War," in *Up South: Stories, Studies, and Letters of This Century's Black Migrations*, ed. Malaika Adero (New York: The New Press, 1993), 2–3.

5.   Arna Bontemps and Jack Conroy, "The Exodus Train," in ibid., 206–15; Stewart E. Tolnay and E. M. Beck, "Rethink-

ing the Role of Racial Violence in the Great Migration," in *Black Exodus: The Great Migration from the American South,* ed. Alferdteen Harrison (Jackson: University Press of Mississippi, 1991), 22; Lemann, *Promised Land,* 16.

6. Lemann, *Promised Land,* 40–41, 57–58; Emmett J. Scott, *Negro Migration during the War* (1920; reprint, New York: Arno Press and the New York Times, 1969), 153–55.

7. Mandle, *Not Slave, Not Free,* 78–89.

8. James H. Madison, *Indiana through Tradition and Change: A History of the Hoosier State and Its People, 1920–1945* (Indianapolis: Indiana Historical Society, 1982), 2–7.

9. James J. Divita, "Demography and Ethnicity," in *The Encyclopedia of Indianapolis,* eds. David J. Bodenhamer and Robert G. Barrows (Bloomington: Indiana University Press, 1994), 56–57.

10. Emma Lou Thornbrough, *Since Emancipation: A Short History of Indiana Negroes, 1863–1963* ([Indianapolis?]: Indiana Division American Negro Emancipation Centennial Authority, 1963), 16–23.

11. Ibid., 23–24.

12. Nina Mjagkij, "Senate Avenue YMCA," and A'Lelia Perry Bundles, "Walker, Madam C. J.," in *Encyclopedia of Indianapolis,* 1249–50, 1405–6. See also Clyde N. Bolden, "Indiana Avenue: Black Entertainment Boulevard" (master's thesis, University of Cincinnati, 1983), and Amy H. Wilson, "The Swing Era on Indiana Avenue: A Cultural History of Indianapolis' African-American Jazz Scene, 1933–1950" (master's thesis, Indiana University, 1997).

13. Michelle D. Hale, "Indiana Avenue," in *Encyclopedia of Indianapolis,* 730.

14. Susan White, "The Avenue: Where the Black Man Has Always Been King," *Indianapolis* 9, no. 5 (May 1972): 36a.

15. Thornbrough, *Since Emancipation,* 75–76; Leigh Darbee, "Lockefield Gardens," in *Encyclopedia of Indianapolis,* 926–27.

16. Hale, "Indiana Avenue," 731.

17. Ibid.; David N. Baker, "Jazz," in *Encyclopedia of Indianapolis,* 840–43.

18. Hale, "Indiana Avenue," 731; Thornbrough, *Since Emancipation,* 41, 76–77; Divita, "Demography and Ethnicity," 57.

CHAPTER TWO

1. Booth Tarkington, *The Magnificent Ambersons* (Garden City, N.Y.: Doubleday, Page and Co., 1918), 389.

2. M. William Lutholtz, *Grand Dragon: D. C. Stephenson and the Ku Klux Klan in Indiana* (West Lafayette, Ind.: Purdue University Press, 1991), 8–32.

3. Ibid., 40–41.

4. Stanley Warren, "The Evolution of Secondary Schooling for Blacks in Indianapolis, 1869–1930," in *Indiana's African-American Heritage: Essays from* Black History News & Notes, ed. Wilma L. Gibbs (Indianapolis: Indiana Historical Society, 1993), 29–34. Except where noted, the Crispus Attucks story is from this essay.

5. Stanley Warren, "The Other Side of Hoosier Hysteria: Segregation, Sports, and the IHSAA," *Black History News & Notes,* no. 54 (Nov. 1993): 1, 3–8. Except where noted, the story of the integration of the IHSAA is from this essay.

6. Phillip M. Hoose, *Hoosiers: The Fabulous Basketball Life of Indiana,* 2d ed. (Indianapolis: Guild Press of Indiana, 1995), 150–55.

7. *The Indiana High School Athletic Association: Thirty-Ninth Annual Handbook* (Indianapolis: Indiana High School Athletic Association Board of Control, 1942), 148.

8. Kerry D. Marshall, *The Ray Crowe Story: A Legend in High School Basketball* ([Indianapolis]: High School Basketball Cards of America, 1992), 1–22. The basic details of Crowe's career come from this book and interviews with Crowe, Joe Wolfla, Oscar Robertson, Bill Swatts, and Bill Scott.

9. Hoose, *Hoosiers,* 153–55.

10. Marshall, *Ray Crowe Story,* 31.

11. Ibid., 58–59.

12. Ibid., 55.

13. Ibid., 60–61.

14. Ibid., 67.

15. *Indianapolis Recorder,* Mar. 21, 1953; *Indianapolis Star,* Mar. 15, 1953.

16. *Indianapolis Recorder,* Mar. 21, 1953.

17. Ibid.

CHAPTER THREE

1. *Indianapolis Recorder,* Nov. 14, 21, 1953.

2. Ibid., Nov. 21, 1953.

3. Ibid., Nov. 28, 1953.

4. Ibid., Dec. 5, 1953; Kerry D. Marshall, *The Ray Crowe Story: A Legend in High School Basketball* ([Indianapolis]: High School Basketball Cards of America, 1992), 103–4.

5. *Indianapolis Recorder,* Dec. 5, 1953.

6. *Indianapolis Star,* Dec. 9, 1953.

7. *Indianapolis Recorder,* Dec. 12, 1953.

8. *Indianapolis Star,* Dec. 10, 11, 1953.

9. Ibid., Dec. 12, 16, 1953.

10. Ibid., Dec. 16, 17, 1953.

11. Ibid., Dec. 17, 1953.

12. Phillip M. Hoose, *Hoosiers: The Fabulous Basketball Life of Indiana,* 2d ed. (Indianapolis: Guild Press of Indiana, 1995), 182–83; *Indianapolis Star,* Jan. 2, 1954.

13. *Indianapolis Star*, Jan. 3, 1954.

14. Ibid.

15. *Indianapolis Recorder*, Jan. 16, 23, 30, 1954; *Indianapolis Star*, Jan. 23, 24, 27, Feb. 5, 1954.

16. *Indianapolis Recorder*, Feb. 13, 1954.

17. *Indianapolis Star*, Jan. 21, 24, 27, Feb. 6, 1954; *Indianapolis Recorder*, Mar. 20, 1954.

18. *Indianapolis Star*, Feb. 11, 18, 19, 20, 1954; *Indianapolis Recorder*, Feb. 20, 1954.

19. *Indianapolis Recorder*, Feb. 13, 27, 1954.

20. Ibid., Feb. 13, Mar. 6, 1954.

21. *Indianapolis Star*, Feb. 27, 28, 1954.

22. Ibid., Feb. 28, 1954.

23. *Indianapolis Recorder*, Mar. 6, 1954.

24. Ibid., Mar. 13, 20, 1954.

25. *Indianapolis Star*, Mar. 7, 1954; *Indianapolis Recorder*, Mar. 13, 1954.

26. Hoose, *Hoosiers*, 121–41; Greg Guffey, *The Greatest Basketball Story Ever Told: The Milan Miracle, Then and Now* (Bloomington: Indiana University Press, 1993), 8–59.

27. *Indianapolis Star*, Mar. 8, 1954.

28. Ibid., Mar. 10, 1954; Guffey, *Greatest Basketball Story Ever Told*, 80–82.

29. *Indianapolis Star*, Mar. 14, 1954.

30. Hoose, *Hoosiers*, 132.

31. Guffey, *Greatest Basketball Story Ever Told*, 83.

32. Ibid., 96–103; Hoose, *Hoosiers*, 137–38.

CHAPTER FOUR

1. S. L. Price, "Whatever Happened to the White Athlete?" *Sports Illustrated*, Dec. 8, 1997, 38.

2. This discussion of white attitudes toward black athletes has been adapted from the author's work in Randy Roberts and James S. Olson, *Winning Is the Only Thing: Sports in America since 1945* (Baltimore: Johns Hopkins University Press, 1989), 25–45; see also John M. Hoberman, *Darwin's Athletes: How Sport Has Damaged Black America and Preserved the Myth of Race* (Boston: Houghton Mifflin, 1997).

3. Robert Peterson, *Only the Ball Was White* (Englewood Cliffs, N.J.: Prentice-Hall, 1970), 149–53, 203–4.

4. *Indianapolis Recorder,* Oct. 30, Nov. 13, 1954.

5. Ibid., Nov. 20, 1954.

6. Ibid., Nov. 27, 1954.

7. *Indianapolis Times,* Dec. 8, 1954.

8. *Indianapolis Recorder,* Nov. 27, 1954.

9. Ibid., Dec. 4, 1954.

10. Ibid.; Nelson George, *Elevating the Game: Black Men and Basketball* (New York: HarperCollins, 1992), 68–71.

11. George, *Elevating the Game,* 69.

12. *Indianapolis Recorder,* Dec. 4, 1954.

13. Ibid., Dec. 11, 1954.

14. *Indianapolis Times,* Dec. 16, 1954.

15. *Indianapolis News,* Dec. 16, 1954; *Indianapolis Recorder,* Dec. 18, 1954.

16. Kerry D. Marshall, *The Ray Crowe Story: A Legend in High School Basketball* ([Indianapolis]: High School Basketball Cards of America, 1992), 122–23.

17. Ibid., 123.

18. *Indianapolis Times,* Jan. 6, 1955.

19. *Indianapolis Recorder,* Jan. 8, 15, 22, 29, 1955; *Indianapolis Star,* Jan. 13, 19, 23, 1955; *Indianapolis Times,* Jan. 23, 1955.

20. *Indianapolis Recorder,* Feb. 5, 1955.

21. For details of the Attucks-Connersville game see *Indianapolis Recorder,* Feb. 5, 12, 1955; *Indianapolis News,* Feb. 7, 1955; *Indianapolis Times,* Feb. 6, 1955; Phillip M. Hoose, *Hoosiers: The Fabulous Basketball Life of Indiana,* 2d ed. (Indianapolis: Guild Press of Indiana, 1995), 185.

22. *Indianapolis Recorder,* Feb. 12, 1955.

23. Ibid.

24. Ibid., Feb. 26, 1955; *Indianapolis Star,* Feb. 18, 1955.

25. *Indianapolis Star,* Feb. 14, 1955.

26. Ibid., Jan. 22, 1955.

27. *Indianapolis Recorder,* Feb. 26, 1955.

CHAPTER FIVE

1. *Indianapolis Recorder,* Feb. 19, 1955.

2. Ibid., Feb. 26, 1955.

3. Ibid., Mar. 5, 1955.

4. *Indianapolis Times,* Mar. 6, 1955.

5. Ibid.

6. *Indianapolis Recorder,* Mar. 12, 1955.

7. For details of the game see *Indianapolis Star,* Mar. 13, 14, 1955; *Indianapolis Times,* Mar. 13, 1955; *Indianapolis Recorder,* Mar. 19, 1955.

8. *Indianapolis Recorder,* Mar. 19, 1955.

9. *Indianapolis Star,* Mar. 13, 1955.

10. Ibid., Mar. 14, 1955.

11. Phillip M. Hoose, *Hoosiers: The Fabulous Basketball Life of Indiana,* 2d ed. (Indianapolis: Guild Press of Indiana, 1995), 187; Nelson George, *Elevating the Game: Black Men and Basketball* (New York: HarperCollins, 1992), 120; Rosie Cheatham Mickey, "Russell Adrian Lane: Biography of an Urban Negro School Administrator," (Ph.D. diss., University of Akron, 1983), 153.

12. Hoose, *Hoosiers,* 187.

13. *Indianapolis Recorder,* Mar. 19, 1955.

14. *Indianapolis Star,* Mar. 18, 1955.

15. Ibid.

16. Ibid., Mar. 20, 1955.

17. *Indianapolis Recorder,* Mar. 26, 1955.

18. Ibid.

19. Ibid.

20. *Indianapolis Star,* Mar. 20, 1955.

21. Hoose, *Hoosiers,* 188.

22. *Indianapolis Recorder,* Mar. 26, 1955.

23. Ibid.

24. Ibid.

25. Ibid., Apr. 2, 1955.

CHAPTER SIX

1. *Indianapolis Star,* Nov. 16, 1955.

2. *Indianapolis Recorder,* Nov. 19, 1955.

3. *Indianapolis Times,* Nov. 17, 1955.

4. Ibid.

5. *Indianapolis Recorder,* Nov. 19, 1955.

6. Ibid., Nov. 26, 1955.

7. *Indianapolis Times,* Nov. 13, 1955; *Indianapolis Recorder,* Nov. 12, 1955.

8. Kerry D. Marshall, *The Ray Crowe Story: A Legend in High School Basketball* ([Indianapolis]: High School Basketball Cards of America, 1992), 140.

9. *Indianapolis Recorder,* Nov. 12, 1955.

10. *Indianapolis Times,* Nov. 19, 1955.

11. *Indianapolis Star,* Nov. 20, 1955; *Indianapolis Times,* Nov. 20, 1955.

12. *Indianapolis Recorder,* Nov. 26, 1955.

13. Ibid.; *Indianapolis Star,* Nov. 20, 1955, Jan. 8, 1956.

14. *Indianapolis Recorder,* Dec. 10, 1955.

15. Ibid.; *Indianapolis Star,* Dec. 16, 1955.

16. *Indianapolis Recorder,* Dec. 24, 1955; *Indianapolis Star,* Dec. 18, 1955. Williams incorrectly added Robertson's total points and came up with a figure of 211 instead of 191. He did correctly figure the average to be 27 points for seven games.

17. *Indianapolis Star,* Dec. 28, 1955.

18. Ibid., Dec. 29, 1955.

19. *Indianapolis Times,* Dec. 30, 1955; *Indianapolis Recorder,* Jan. 7, 1956.

20. *Indianapolis Star,* Jan. 1, 1956; *Indianapolis Recorder,* Jan. 7, 1956.

21. *Indianapolis Star,* Jan. 1, 1956; *Indianapolis Recorder,* Dec. 10, 1955.

22. *Indianapolis Recorder,* Dec. 31, 1955.

23. Taylor Branch, *Parting the Waters: America in the King Years, 1954–63* (New York: Simon and Schuster, 1988), 128–42; William H. Chafe, *The Unfinished Journey: America since World War II* (New York: Oxford University Press, 1986), 162.

24. Chafe, *Unfinished Journey,* 164.

25. *Indianapolis Recorder,* Jan. 14, 1956.

26. *Indianapolis Star,* Jan. 16, 1956.

27. *Indianapolis Recorder,* Jan. 21, 1956; *Indianapolis Star,* Jan. 16, 1956.

28. *Indianapolis Star,* Jan. 18, 1956; *Indianapolis Recorder,* Jan. 21, 1956; *Indianapolis Times,* Jan. 18, 1956.

29. *Indianapolis Star,* Jan. 19, 1956.

30. *Indianapolis Star,* Jan. 22, 1956.

31. *Indianapolis Recorder,* Jan. 28, 1956.

32. *Indianapolis Star,* Jan. 22, 1956; *Indianapolis Times,* Jan. 18, 1956.

33. *Indianapolis Recorder,* Feb. 4, 1956.

34. Ibid., Feb. 11, 1956.

35. *Indianapolis Star,* Feb. 2, 1956.

36. Ibid., Feb. 9, 1956.

37. *Indianapolis Recorder,* Feb. 18, 1956.

38. Ibid.; *Indianapolis Star,* Feb. 12, 1956; *Indianapolis Times,* Feb. 12, 1956.

39. *Indianapolis Recorder,* Feb. 18, 1956.

40. Ibid., Feb. 25, 1956.

CHAPTER SEVEN

1. *Indianapolis Star,* Feb. 14, 16, 21, 1956.

2. *Indianapolis Recorder,* Feb. 18, 1956.

3. Ibid., Mar. 3, 1956.

4. *Indianapolis Times,* Feb. 21, 22, 1956.

5. *Indianapolis Recorder,* Mar. 3, 1956.

6. Ibid.

7. *Indianapolis Star,* Feb. 27, 1956.

8. *Indianapolis Recorder,* Mar. 3, 1956.

9. Ibid.

10. *Indianapolis Star,* Feb. 26, 1956.

11. *Indianapolis News,* Mar. 2, 1956; *Indianapolis Star,* Feb. 29, Mar. 3, 1956.

12. *Indianapolis Recorder,* Mar. 10, 1956.

13. Ibid.; *Indianapolis Star,* Mar. 4, 1956.

14. *Indianapolis Recorder,* Mar. 10, 1956; *Indianapolis Star,* Mar. 5, 1956.

15. *Indianapolis Star,* Mar. 4, 5, 1956.

16. Ibid., Mar. 16, 1956.

17. Ibid., Mar. 7, 1956; *Connersville (Ind.) News-Examiner,* Mar. 5, 1956.

18. *Indianapolis Star,* Mar. 7, 9, 10, 1956.

19. Ibid., Mar. 11, 1956; *Indianapolis Recorder,* Mar. 17, 1956.

20. *Indianapolis Recorder,* Mar. 17, 1956.

21. *Indianapolis Star,* Mar. 17, 1956.

22. Ibid.

23. *Indianapolis Recorder,* Mar. 17, 1956.

24. *Indianapolis Star,* Mar. 17, 18, 1956.

25. Ibid., Mar. 18, 1956; *Indianapolis Recorder,* Mar. 24, 1956.

26. *Indianapolis Recorder,* Mar. 24, 1956.

27. *Indianapolis Star,* Mar. 18, 1956.

28. Ibid., Mar. 17, 19, 1956.

29. Ibid., Mar. 18, 19, 1956.

30. *Indianapolis Times,* Mar. 18, 1956.

31. Nelson George, *Elevating the Game: Black Men and Basketball* (New York: HarperCollins, 1992), 122–23.

32. *Indianapolis Star,* Mar. 18, 1956; *Indianapolis Recorder,* Mar. 24,1956; *Indianapolis Times,* Mar. 18, 1956.

33. *Indianapolis Recorder,* Mar. 24, 1956.

34. A. E. Housman, "To an Athlete Dying Young," in *A Shropshire Lad* (1896; reprinted in *The Collected Poems of A. E. Housman,* New York: Holt, Rinehart and Winston, 1965), 32–33.

35. *Indianapolis Star,* Mar. 18, 1956.

36. Ibid., Mar. 18, 19, 1956.

37. *Indianapolis Recorder,* Mar. 31, 1956; *Indianapolis News,* Mar. 19, 1956.

38. *Indianapolis Recorder,* Mar. 24, 1956.

39. Ibid.

40. Ibid.

EPILOGUE

1. Phillip M. Hoose, *Hoosiers: The Fabulous Basketball Life of Indiana,* 2d ed. (Indianapolis: Guild Press of Indiana, 1995), 111–14.

2. Ibid., 112–14.

3. Ibid., 114.

4. For the Wilt Chamberlain story see Wilt Chamberlain and David Shaw, *Wilt: Just Like Any Other 7-Foot Black Millionaire Who Lives Next Door* (New York: Macmillan; London: Collier Macmillan, 1973), 41–49; Bill Libby, *Goliath: The Wilt Chamberlain Story* (New York: Dodd, Mead, 1977), 26–33.

5. Chamberlain and Shaw, *Wilt,* 48.

6. *Cincinnati Enquirer,* Jan. 7, 1959.

7. Jules Tygiel, *Baseball's Great Experiment: Jackie Robinson and His Legacy* (New York: Oxford University Press, 1983), 304.

8. Reginald C. McGrane, *The University of Cincinnati: A Success Story in Urban Higher Education* (New York: Harper and Row, 1963), 210, 336.

9. *Cincinnati Enquirer,* Jan. 7, 1959.

10. For details of the series see Herb Schwomeyer, *Hoosier Hysteria: A History of Indiana High School Boys Single Class Basketball,* 9th ed. (Greenfield, Ind.: Mitchell-Fleming Printing, 1997), 444–53.

11. *Indianapolis Star,* June 21, 1956; *Indianapolis Recorder,* June 23, 1956.

12. *Indianapolis Star,* June 21, 1956.

13. Ibid., June 24, 1956.

14. Ibid.

15. Ibid., June 25, 1956.

16. Ibid., June 26, 1956.

17.   Ibid., June 27, 1956.

18.   Ibid., June 26, 1956.

19.   Ibid., June 27, 1956.

Bibliographical Essay

This book is based on two primary sources. First, it is grounded in the Indianapolis newspapers of the 1950s. The *Indianapolis Star, Indianapolis News, Indianapolis Times,* and especially *Indianapolis Recorder* devoted hundreds of columns and editorials to the Crispus Attucks Tigers. Nothing can replace their coverage for the day-to-day details of Indiana high school basketball. Second, a series of interviews added depth to the story. Several people I interviewed wished to remain anonymous, but they were less important than the ones who sat for formal, taped interviews. But they all spoke candidly and with passion. I conducted formal interviews with Oscar Robertson, Yvonne Robertson, Bailey Robertson Sr., Ray Crowe, Albert Spurlock, Bill Scott, Edgar Searcy, Bill Swatts, Joe Wolfla, Ray Craft, Vic Klinker, Glenn Sample, and Ed Jucker.

Other books and articles helped on different aspects of the story. Indiana and Crispus Attucks basketball is covered in Phillip M. Hoose, *Hoosiers: The Fabulous Basketball Life of Indiana,* 2d ed. (Indianapolis: Guild Press of Indiana, 1995); Bob Williams, *Hoosier Hysteria: Indiana High School Basketball* (South Bend, Ind.: Hardwood Press, 1997); and Kerry D. Marshall, *The*

Ray Crowe Story: A Legend in High School Basketball ([Indianapolis]: High School Basketball Cards of America, 1992). The game of the 1950s is given some context in Albert G. Applin, "From Muscular Christianity to the Market Place: The History of Men's and Boy's Basketball in the United States, 1891–1957" (Ph.D. diss., University of Massachusetts, 1982); Charles Rosen, *Scandals of '51: How Gamblers Almost Killed College Basketball* (New York: Holt, Rinehart and Winston, 1978); Stanley Cohen, *The Game They Played* (New York: Farrar, Straus and Giroux, 1977); and Nelson George, *Elevating the Game: Black Men and Basketball* (New York: HarperCollins, 1992).

The history of Crispus Attucks High School is well covered by Stanley Warren in *Crispus Attucks High School: "Hail to the Green, Hail to the Gold"* (Virginia Beach, Va.: Donning, 1998); "The Evolution of Secondary Schooling for Blacks in Indianapolis, 1869–1930," in *Indiana's African-American Heritage: Essays from Black History News & Notes,* ed. Wilma Gibbs (Indianapolis: Indiana Historical Society, 1993), 29–34; and "The Other Side of Hoosier Hysteria: Segregation, Sports, and the IHSAA," *Black History News & Notes,* no. 54 (Nov. 1993): 1, 3–8. For the history of African Americans in Indiana and Indianapolis see James H. Madison, *Indiana through Tradition and Change: A History of the Hoosier State and Its People, 1920–1945* (Indianapolis: Indiana Historical Society, 1982); Emma Lou Thornbrough, *Since Emancipation: A Short History of Indiana Negroes, 1863–1963* ([Indianapolis?]: Indiana Division American Negro Emancipation Centennial Authority, 1963); Susan White, "The Avenue: Where the Black Man Has Always Been King," *Indianapolis* 9, no. 5 (May 1972): 32a–36a, 73a–74a; Clyde N. Bolden, "Indiana Avenue: Black Entertainment Boulevard" (master's thesis, University of Cincinnati, 1983); Amy H. Wilson, "The Swing Era on Indiana Avenue: A Cultural History of Indianapolis'

African-American Jazz Scene, 1933–1950" (master's thesis, Indiana University, 1997); and David J. Bodenhamer and Robert G. Barrows, eds., *The Encyclopedia of Indianapolis* (Bloomington: Indiana University Press, 1994).

Finally, the subject of race and sport are explored in Randy Roberts and James S. Olson, *Winning Is the Only Thing: Sports in America since 1945* (Baltimore: Johns Hopkins University Press, 1989) and John M. Hoberman, *Darwin's Athletes: How Sport Has Damaged Black America and Preserved the Myth of Race* (Boston: Houghton Mifflin, 1997).

Index